Bound and Gagged

Bound and Gagged

*Pornography and the
Politics of Fantasy in America*

Laura Kipnis

Grove Press/New York

Published simultaneously in Canada
Printed in the United States of America
FIRST EDITION

Kipnis, Laura.
    Bound and gagged: pornography and the politics of fantasy in America / by Laura Kipnis. — 1st ed.
       p.   cm.
    Includes bibliographical references.
    ISBN 0-8021-1584-5
    1. Pornography—United States. 2. Pornography—Social aspects—United States. I. Title.
    HQ472.U6K56 1996   363.4'7'0973—dc20   95-39193

DESIGN BY LAURA HAMMOND HOUGH

Grove Press
841 Broadway
New York, NY 10003

10 9 8 7 6 5 4 3 2 1

Contents

Preface

We're lately in the midst of a massive wave of social hysteria focused on pornography, which spills over into art and other cultural spheres. Through a strange-bedfellows alliance of the religious right, the feminist right, and cultural conservatives, pornography has become an all-purpose whipping person. From the Spenglerian scoldings about cultural decline to holy-roller excoriations about the pornographer-terrorist-homosexual lobby, you'd think that pornography has single-handedly brought down Western culture. At the same time, for certain feminists, pornography has become a convenient way to symbolize the omnipresence of rape and violence to women.

The panicked tenor of this new moral bloc has filtered down through the social structure, and the frenzy doesn't stop with pornography proper. Museum curators are put on trial. Parents are arrested for taking naked pictures of their kids. Sex and AIDS education are under assault. The National Endowment for the Arts is defunded by Congress after charges that it supports "pornographic art." Legislation is under way to police the Internet for dirty pictures. At the same time, mainstream culture like movies and TV, advertising, pop music, not to mention high art, are borrowing pornographic explicitness, making the distinctions between the pornographic and the nonpornographic harder and harder to maintain, if they were ever tenable at all.

This book means to offer a different footing for debates about pornography. Its position is that the differences between pornography and other forms of culture are less meaningful than their similarities. Pornography *is* a form of cultural expression, and though it's transgressive, disruptive, and hits below the belt —in more ways than one—it's an essential form of contemporary national culture. It's also a genre devoted to fantasy, and its fantasies traverse a range of motifs beyond the strictly sexual. Sex is pornography's vehicle, and also its mode of distraction, but coursing through pornography's dimly lit corridors are far larger issues. Abandon your prejudices about what kind of language is appropriate to serious philosophical inquiry, and you can see that within the staged, mythic world of pornography a number of philosophical questions are posed, though couched in a low idiom: questions concerning the social compact and the price of repression, questions about what men are (and aren't), what women are (and aren't), questions about how sexuality and gender roles are performed, about class, aesthetics, utopia, rebellion, power, desire, and commodification.

Reading between the bodies, you can also see the way that pornography lends itself as a form, in fairly mobile ways, to local necessities for expression of what's routinely muzzled from other public forums. Like pornography of the past, from Boccaccio to Rabelais to Sade, it gets appropriated as a form of speech and deployed around subjects and issues that are the most "unspeakable," the most buried, but also the most politically and culturally significant.[1] Or this is what you'll see if you give up insisting on the importance of high-minded language and grim-faced humorlessness to the task of philosophical or political engagement. And if you step back, just momentarily, from whatever dismay pornography may cause you. But if we've learned anything from the artistic avant-garde—besides the imperative to question the automatic reverence accorded high seriousness—it's that administering shocks to the bourgeois sensibility looks, in historical retrospect at least, like an important cultural project. Savor those shocks.

What follows is not an exhaustive survey of all existing pornography, but a strategic and selective one. Pornography is immensely popular: its annual multi-billion-dollar sales rival the gross revenues of the three major TV networks combined. While magazines like *Playboy* and *Penthouse* have high visibility and even a certain degree of respectability, the focus here is on less frequently discussed pornographic subgenres that I expect will fluster all the conventional platitudes about porn (it's all about violence, it's all about debasing women). We'll cover the gamut, from S&M to transvestite personal ads, to fat pornography, to *Hustler* magazine, to geriatric porn, infantilism, and tickling. Peripheral as they may seem at first glance, these pornographic subgenres distill many of our most pivotal cultural preoccupations.

Center stage within all pornography is the question of fantasy and its social meanings. But let's be quite clear: this isn't some abstract, theoretical concern. Without any public discussion of the issue whatsoever, the state has now taken the position that fantasizing about something illegal *is* illegal, and pursues prosecutions of the citizenry on that basis. As the opening chapter details, two Virginia men were sent to prison for over thirty years for having the wrong fantasies, and for being incau-

tious enough to verbalize them in the wrong place. The notion
that you can be imprisoned for thought crimes strikes most of
us as something out of Orwell or a sci-fi dystopia, but this turns
out to be the world we now inhabit. If public policy and policing procedures are enacted on the basis of the most simplistic
assumptions about the role of fantasy in the human psyche (that
fantasy is synonymous with intent, for instance), this imperils a
basic form of freedom, as well as the available modes of political expression.

This book is not a rehash of the debates between antipornography feminists and anticensorship liberals: it endeavors to
make an argument about pornography whose terms aren't dictated in advance by its opponents. This has proven difficult for
the majority of "anti-antipornography" writers, because the positions of antiporn feminists Catharine MacKinnon and Andrea
Dworkin have so dominated the debates and so influenced public policy discussions. Call me a feminist apostate, but I say
there's more to pornography than a celebration of gender oppression, and limiting the discussion to that issue alone closes the
door before things get interesting. If pornography offends women
(or some women) more than it offends men (most men?) the
question, What does it mean to be offended? needs to be put in
front of us. But this is also not simply a "pro-sex" argument: I
don't see in pornography the key that will unleash our reserves
of unrepressed animal sexuality. Certainly everyone's entitled
to better orgasms—wherever and whenever they can be had—
but once you've accomplished that, there's still the issue of what
pornography means as a form of culture, and why it's so meaningful *to* our culture, especially now.[2]

Whether pornography should or shouldn't exist is pretty
much beside the point. It does exist, and it's not going to go away.
Why it exists, what it has to say, and who pornography thinks
it's talking to, are more interesting questions than all these

doomed, dreary attempts to debate it, regulate it, or protest it. Just what is pornography's grip on the cultural imagination?

Debates over pornography have generally seesawed back and forth over the same now-familiar issues. The First Amendment and freedom of the press versus putting a leash on obscenity. Women's right to be protected from offensive images versus sexual freedom and expressiveness. These arguments have become tedious because they evade what's really at stake in pornography with a barrage of smoke screens and circumlocutions, routinely reaching the heights of hypocrisy and the depths of logic, often simultaneously. Suddenly cultural conservatives start sounding like ardent feminists ("Pornography exploits women!"), feminists start sounding like autocratic patriarchs ("Women in the sex industry are incompetent to make informed career choices"), and staunch Republican free-marketeers become anti–big business ("They're just out to make a buck at the expense of our children").

Who's to say whether performing sexual labor is a worse or more dehumanizing job than manual labor or service-industry labor or working on an assembly line or waitressing, other than the person doing it? And let's not get too romantic about how much choice the labor market allows anyone, or how great working conditions are across the board. It's not as if we have all the vocational choices in the world: "Should I be a porn queen or . . . president of IBM?" If you get teary-eyed about exploited pornography workers and haven't thought much about international garment workers, or poultry workers—to name just two of the countless and quotidian examples of those with less than wonderful working conditions—then maybe your analysis needs some work. And some consistency. Contrary to some feminists, I think we have to operate on the basis that women *are* capable of making informed decisions about how to conduct their lives, and recognize at the same time that labor under capitalism, is, by its nature, exploited. The changes that are happening in sex industry work are being made from within, through organization.[3] It always seems a little disingenuous when those who could care less about the violence of global capitalism, and think labor unions need to be taught who's boss, become raving socialists when it comes to pornography. (Incidentally, no one seems too worried about men being exploited by the porn industry, which says something about just how beset by stereotypes these discussions are.) None of this is a justification for the pornography industry; it simply points out that it's not exceptional. If you want to cap corporate profit, institute worker self-management, end alienated labor, or even dismantle capitalism altogether, I'm right behind you. But not if your revolutionary zeal is confined to this one particular industry.

Pornography *is* a business—as is all our popular entertainment—which has attained popularity because it finds ways of articulating things its audiences care about. When it doesn't, we turn it off. If you start out from the supposition that no complexity could possibly reside in "lower" forms of culture, in commercial culture, you will, of course, miss the complexity that does reside there. Pornography may indeed be the sexuality of a consumer society. It may have a certain emptiness, a lack of interior, a disconnectedness—as does so much of our popular culture. And our high culture. (As does much of what passes for political discourse these days, too.) But that doesn't mean that pornography isn't, at the same time, an expressive form. It speaks to its audience because it's thoroughly astute about who we are underneath the social veneer, astute about the costs of cultural conformity and the discontent at the core of routinized lives and normative sexuality. Its audience is drawn to it because it provides opportunities—perhaps in coded, sexualized forms, but opportunities nonetheless—for a range of effects, pleasures, and desires; for the experience of transgression, utopian aspirations, sadness, optimism, loss; and even the most primary long-ings for love and plenitude.[4]

It's *this* nakedness that may have something do with the contempt—and perhaps the embarrassment—with which pornography is so routinely regarded. And the ambivalence. However, I'm suggesting that we regard pornography more creatively—and more discerningly—which, as the following chapters describe, is how it regards us.[5]

Bound and Gagged

One

Fantasy in America:
The United States v.
Daniel Thomas DePew

What kind of society sends its citizens to prison for their fantasies?

When an undercover San Jose police officer calling himself "Bobby" phoned Daniel DePew in Alexandria, Virginia, to suggest that they had "mutual interests" and invited him to his hotel for dinner, DePew, ever the optimist—and thinking that he'd been beckoned to a blind date with an out-of-town prospect—showered, put on a pair of tight jeans, and drove himself to the Dulles Airport Marriott. Twenty-eight at the time, DePew was a systems control engineer at a high-tech electronics company; he was also, in his off-hours, a well-known habitué of the gay sadomasochistic subculture of the Washington, D.C., area. Subcultures have their own private languages, along with shared sets of rules and codes of behavior that members employ: to DePew, when Bobby said "mutual interests" it meant S&M sex. It wasn't unusual for him to meet people over the phone and get together to explore fantasies, maybe have some kind of scene—which often included verbalizing elaborate and violent fictional scenarios. Fantasy was a major component of DePew's sexual universe. What DePew didn't know was that what Bobby had in mind was that Dan play the role of executioner in a snuff film that Bobby was scripting, that Bobby was inviting Dan to his hotel room to discuss kidnapping and murdering a child, and that Bobby was working for the government. Our government.

What follows is a case study about odd, disturbing, and violent sexual fantasies, but just whose fantasies were they? Daniel DePew was sentenced to thirty-three years in prison for sitting around a hotel room and trading detailed kinky fantasies with two undercover cops who'd invited him there in the first place, and who spurred him on by sharing their own equally kinky fantasies, while a team of FBI agents listened eagerly in the next room. The cops and FBI agents are still roaming the streets; DePew is serving out his sentence in a federal prison. The fantasies never progressed beyond the realm of fantasy. This is a story about a crime that never happened. There was no victim. It's also a story that wouldn't have taken place without a couple of zealous law enforcement agents prodding a couple of tragically over-susceptible men to scratch open their psychic scars and plumb their darkest fantasies while the tape recorders rolled—like Kafkaesque state-sponsored psychotherapy—with every free association captured as evidence for a future trial.[1]

United States v. DePew was the first prosecution nationwide involving sex-related computer bulletin boards, which is where a Richmond, Virginia, real estate agent named Dean Lambey inadvertently picked up a San Jose undercover cop and proceeded to lead Daniel DePew, whom he'd met only once, into the setup. These bulletin boards, and their successors on the Internet, were, briefly, an unregulated space for all manner of nonconstrained expression, whether political, sexual, creative, or just weird. These days any small-town cop with a modem and a nose for sin can log on to the Internet and set about electronically policing the sexual proclivities of the nation. And following the case of a California couple sentenced to prison after an undercover Memphis postal inspector received their pornographic images over the Internet, Net hounds around the country are faced with the task of ensuring that their fantasy lives conform to the community standards of the Bible Belt, or risk prosecution. At the same time, these prosecutions are conducted haphazardly and rulings are contradictory: despite massive publicity about the 1995 arrest of a University of Michigan student after he published a violent fantasy about another student on a computer bulletin board and discussed similar fantasies through E-mail, the case was dismissed by a federal judge (after the student had spent a month in jail) who decided that the story and the E-mails were merely tasteless fiction. Federal legislation is now pending to criminalize sexually explicit speech and images on the Internet—ironically, as an amendment to a bill otherwise deregulating the telecommunications industry.

It's inevitable that the Internet will increasingly be used for entrapment purposes, as was the case with DePew and Lambey. The rationale for this expansion of law enforcement into the fantasies of the citizenry comes cloaked as the all-too-necessary responsibility of protecting children from perverts. The subject of child sexual abuse is so emotionally charged these days that little rational discussion of the topic is possible. Pedophilia is the new evil empire of the domestic imagination: now that communism has been defanged, it seems to occupy a similar metaphysical status as the evil of all evils, with similar anxiety about security from infiltration, the similar under-the-bed fear that "they" walk among us undetected—fears that are not entirely groundless, but not entirely rational either. (And predictably, the FBI once again plays a key role in ferreting out wrongdoing.)

Although the fact is that children are at far greater risk of abuse, violence, and murder by their own parents than anyone else, cultural panic about child safety attaches far disproportionately to the monster figure of the pedophile stranger-abductor. The missing children campaign of the early 1980s spawned a national mythology that a million children a year were being abducted by murderous perverts. These figures have been widely debunked: the vast majority of missing children are runaways or abducted in custody battles, which was never mentioned on the back of all those milk cartons featuring their haunting portraits. A small fraction of these cases are stranger abductions. The Justice Department estimates 200 to 300 stranger abductions a year (a child taken overnight or longer) and, of these, a fluctuating rate of 50 to 150 murders yearly.

Of course, it's the monstrosity of these crimes rather than their frequency that makes this such an archetypal scene of horror, but despite the terror and dread these cases generate, they're rare compared to family violence (and especially rare compared to other far more routine household dangers to children). As Kenneth Lanning, special supervisory agent at the FBI Academy's Behavioral Science Unit in Quantico, Virginia, puts it, "In the two months that you put all this energy and these resources into one child who's been abducted, two hundred kids are murdered by their mother or father."[2] The cultural preference to fixate on bizarre tales of murderous rings of pedophile-pornographers rather than the mundane and even more horrifying truth of parental violence is, however, unswayable; given these very vocal public sentiments, the pressure is on law enforcement agencies to perform the impossible task of ensuring that these crimes don't happen. That is, to hunt down stranger-pedophiles before they commit crimes. And if, increasingly, their lair is believed to be that unregulated den of perversity, the Internet, it's probably because it's a less impossible territory to police than the nondigital universe. Even if there's the occasional trumped-up charge or manufactured crime, with every widely publicized arrest comes the reassurance that law enforcement agencies have the threat under control, and no one is inclined to look too closely at the particulars. There may now be more attention devoted to family violence than in the past, but as long as the stranger-pedophile can provide a public alibi for violence to children, deflecting attention from where it apparently needs to be deflected, there seems to be a public compact to keep reviving and reinventing the stranger-pedophile threat.

Fantasy is ever present, particularly when it comes to the type of issues evoked in the DePew case. Mainstream culture constructs elaborate fantasies about what it purports it's not—subcultural, foreign, pornographic, violent—which propel, and are enacted in, these highly publicized rituals of control and punishment, policing and mastery. (You can see the control fantasies at work in the cultural fascination with policing as well, which, not unlike other purity rituals—compulsive handwashing comes to mind—desires to excise contamination once and for all. If only you could scrub hard enough.) The overarching fantasy is that the powerfully monstrous bad thing is somewhere else, that it can be caged, and most crucially, that it's "other." Violence isn't here, it's *there*. No, over *there*. Not in the family, but in that Satanic cult disguised as a daycare center; not the criminal justice system, but in the psychopathic stranger. Violence never has a history; it's born from itself, residing in the random and the anomalous, not the mundane and the everyday. Not in us, but in Daniel DePew.[3]

Fantasy permeated all levels of the DePew case, because as a culture, we're never more beset by fantasy than in our assertions about the purity of our own motives, and in our fantastical belief in our own capacity for rationality.

If there's little serious cultural attention devoted to interrogating questions of fantasy—aside from psychoanalysis, that dying lore (killed off by more cost-effective ways of understanding the human psyche, like psychopharmacology)—there's even less serious cultural attention devoted to violent fantasy, despite the fact that, as media pundits never tire of bemoaning, they percolate throughout our popular culture. But violent fantasies aren't only the province of the mass media—governments have them as well, projecting them onto the citizenry.[4] (And the rest of the time, onto other nations.) When the violence question does arise, convenient clichés and convenient scapegoats occupy our attention: mass media is the culprit, especially the pornography industry. And the state keeps mounting expensive commissions and hearings to prove it. Despite the fact that pornography is far less violent than run-of-the-mill popular culture, through the tireless efforts of antiporn feminists and cultural conservatives, violence and pornography are now firmly linked in what passes for debate on the subject, and against all evidence to the contrary—even Women Against Pornography estimates that only 6 percent of pornography is violent.[5]

But what a violent fantasy means in any particular instance is far from predictable; where any particular fantasizer's identifications lie is up for grabs. We view culture, and popular culture, from the vantage point of complicated idiosyncratic private histories, including the formative experience of having often felt powerless and victimized—how can you have been a child and not have felt this? Questions of power, vulnerability, control, and victimhood are raw and tender regions. The entire terrain is laden with projection and denial, including all our facile assumptions that *other* people invariably take pleasure in identifying with the aggression in any imaginary violent scenario. This vastly undercomplicates anyone's imaginative investment in these scenes, because these kinds of experiences are blurred and conflicting: it's possible—it's even routine—to experience contrary emotions simultaneously. Psyches are complicated things.

If the meanings of particular fantasy scenarios to particular viewers aren't simply black and white, if it's impossible to say with any reliability what person X or Y experiences when viewing or constructing a violent fantasy, imagine the conceptual and evidentiary mess when the criminal justice system is called on to take up such labyrinthine matters—if a group of twelve jurors is asked to determine the relation of fantasy to reality, or determine when fantasizing about doing something illegal becomes illegal, or when fantasy becomes intent. How can twelve strangers, caught up in their own fantasies, their own histories, possibly determine *anything* about someone else's fantasy life, particularly when the fantasies strike them as repugnant? Yet a Virginia jury in the DePew case deliberated a fast four hours before declaring that fantasy *is* intent. Beyond a reasonable doubt. The relation of fantasy to reality is fairly tangled to say the least: the entire discipline of psychoanalysis is devoted to unraveling it (and has spent about the last hundred years trying to do so), making a four-hour verdict on the question seem, perhaps, precipitous.

Pornography—like members of sexual subcultures—provides a highly useful set of cultural alibis. Focusing on either, or both, deflects attention from matters upon which the culture prefers not to dwell. Panic-button issues like rape and child molestation don't invite critical thought but rather fear, and fear is available to be mobilized, as populist politicians know so well. If rape and child molestation fail to produce sufficient panic, antipornography activists (having populist ambitions) have further upped the ante by insistently linking pornography to *snuff films*—films in which someone is, supposedly, killed on camera. Catharine MacKinnon, the country's leading antiporn feminist, is fond of remarking that pornography is a continuum on which the end point is the snuff film. Or as she puts it in her stump speech: "Snuff films cast a light on the rest of pornography that shows it for what it is: that it's about the annihilation of women, the destruction of women, the murder and killing of women—in which murder and killing are just the end point that all the rest of pornography is a movement toward."[6]

There's some question, though, whether snuff films actually exist, or are just another cultural myth. Rumors of vast underground snuff film rings began circulating in the mid-1970s following the release of a film called *Snuff,* which ended with a supposed on-camera murder in what purports to be a documentary sequence. A month-long investigation of the film by the Manhattan DA's office ground to a halt when the quite live "victim" was interviewed by police.[7] In fact, no law enforcement agency has ever come across a snuff film. MacKinnon claims to have seen snuff films herself, but refuses to reveal her sources "for reasons of security."[8] Justice Department and FBI officials say they've never seen one. Even U.S. Attorney Henry Hudson, chair of the 1986 Attorney General's Commission on Pornography—and who will later figure in this story—has said, "As far as I can tell, no snuff films have been recovered in the United States. I don't know that anyone has actually seen one."

A snuff film is one of the most evil things imaginable, but they appear to be just that: imaginary. This doesn't stop them from being a subject of massive cultural fascination; in fact, quite the reverse—it's hard to pick up a gritty urban detective novel in which the hero isn't foiling a well-organized band of depraved snuff film makers. It also didn't stop them from being brandished as the linchpin of the DePew case. Rumors about snuff films usually claim they originated in South America (the advertising slogan for the film *Snuff* was "Made in South America where life is cheap," which may have been the ancestry of the rumor). The foreign origin is important, because insofar as the metaphysics of evil is a recurring feature of the social imagination, and gets mobilized by different symbols at different points in history, it's often the case that the bad, scary thing is symbolized by the outsider. Heretics, witches, Jews, homosexuals, communists, international terrorists, and now pedophiles have all had their day as icons of evil and perversity. The threat comes from elsewhere: not from inside our borders, but from foreign southern places; not from family violence, but from the murderous psychopath with a movie camera. "Witch-hunt" is the term invented to describe the zealous quest to eradicate this kind of threat, which is usually, according to the dictionary, "based on slight, doubtful, or irrelevant evidence." This was certainly the case in *United States* v. *DePew*.

Daniel DePew was not a pedophile. All his sexual partners were adults. Unfortunately, they were all adult men, which is still a crime in the state of Virginia, and was surely not a point in his favor with the Virginia jury or prosecutors. DePew was a tailor-made scapegoat: not only the quintessential outsider, but someone who made no bones about his offbeat sexual preferences. For DePew, sex was a form of private theater, and his sex life was often theatrically violent. The violence was never anything but consensual though, and took place between adults. But the content of his fantasies centered primarily around relations of domination and submission, and included extensive role-playing. Often these roles were of fathers or daddies, and sons or "boys"; however, in DePew's lexicon the term "boy" was a role to be played, *not* a chronological age. But according to federal prosecutors, this role-playing made DePew a potential pedophile. They regarded the violence of his fantasies, and the consensual violence of his sex play, as "evidence" and proof beyond a reasonable doubt—as if this could exist in anything but a psychological cartoon world—that he would, without question, have committed violence against a fictional, nonexistent child. In the stripped-down good-guy, bad-guy psychological universe invented by U.S. prosecutors, where fantasy equals intent, and role-playing makes it real, how many thousands of new prisons—each the size of Texas—would it take to hold our new criminal class?

DePew is serving out his sentence at Ray Brook federal prison in upstate New York, a medium-security prison. This is the sixth prison he's been in, largely because every time there's publicity about his case—the publicity tends to be sensationalistic—he gets beat up by other prisoners and then transferred. Consequently he routinely refuses interview requests, and he had some initial reluctance to talk to me. Once he agreed, though, he seemed extraordinarily trusting. I had some ambivalence about this trust: it's his very incautiousness and lack of guile that have landed him where he is. DePew is tall and well built, with a neatly trimmed brownish red beard and pleasant features. Intelligent and likable, he has an open, eager-to-please air and a sort of cheerful, make-the-best-of-things demeanor. He was quite solicitous of me. We met in a room with floor-to-ceiling picture windows overlooking a prison courtyard populated with prisoners strolling between buildings, and once in a while male prisoners stopped to gawk through the glass. "They're not used to seeing women," he would say apologetically, and a bit anxiously. DePew struck me as remarkably without self-pity about the way his life has turned out. Like everyone else who came in contact with him—the judge, the jury forewoman, his defense attorney—I was jarred by the contrast between the gentle quality he projects and the violence of his inner life, which was bared for the world in elaborate detail at his trial.

Research on viewers' responses to pornography has tended to employ social science methodologies: large-scale surveys, measuring physiological responses, setting up weird contrived experiments to measure how volunteers might act in hypothetical situations after being exposed to various kinds of sexual or violent movies. None of this well-funded research explores the question of what fantasies of violence and fantasized sexual violence *mean*: the question of meaning seems to drop straight from sight. What follows takes a diametrically opposite approach: keeping that question resolutely in the foreground and dissecting the meaning of violent sexual fantasy in one man's life. Given how complex, idiosyncratic, and counterintuitive these meanings prove to be, it strongly suggests that no generalization about what violence means or about why viewers are attracted to it is supportable.

Daniel DePew's catastrophe was that his particular fantasies happened to collide with those of the government and criminal justice system. DePew, of course, lost.

It all started when an enterprising San Jose police officer named James Rodrigues, working undercover, placed a message on a California computer bulletin board called CHAOS, which was devoted to gay, sexually explicit conversation. Calling himself "Bobby R.," he wrote, "Subject: Youngsters. Looking for others interested. Hot and need someone. I'll travel if we can set something up. Pics of the real thing better. I like taking pictures and being the star. Hope someone is interested." This was in late February 1989. Dean Ashley Lambey, a real estate agent, then thirty-four, responded, using the name "Dave Ashley": "Your message caught my interest. Think we may have something in common but need to explore more. Want to talk?"

"Bobby" writes back to "Dave Ashley," initiating a discussion of pornography and where to find it, confiding that he has an "extensive personal photo collection and occasional access to 'models.'" It's established that each is interested in young boys, and each assures the other that he's not a postal agent or cop. Bobby implores Dave to keep up the correspondence, as "it's hard to find friends with our interests." He tells Dave that he works in a camp, though he doesn't say what he does there. (This must be straight out of the handbook on how to hook a potential pedophile's interest.)

The correspondence blossoms. The main subject is the impossibility of finding pornography of young boys, which, contrary to mythic reports about vast underground child porn rings, is largely unavailable even if you're zealously searching it out. As Dave complains, "It seems as though there is NO safe source for materials here domestically, unless of course, we want to produce some ourselves." Bobby responds quickly, "What did you have in mind in the way of making our own movies??? Really interested." Dave writes back that he'd only been half-serious, but Bobby continues to press it: "Read that you were fantasizing about the videos. I'm interested if you are??" He lets Dave in on his secret: he works producing pornography for an acquaintance who flies him to different locales to take pictures of "clients and their fantasies," some of which he's managed to keep. He offers, "I'd really like to show some of my stuff off, but would like to keep our conversations up for a little while longer so that I feel more comfortable with the situation."

Over the course of the next three and a half months Bobby painstakingly cultivates and wins Dave's trust, providing a climate of approval and reciprocity for Dave's guilty interest in children. "I think we have mutual ground for a friendship on these grounds," Bobby enthuses, confessing, "I used to think that I was the only person in the world with these feelings and that NO ONE could ever understand how I felt or why different things made me feel the way they did (and still do)." Dave must have felt like he'd stumbled onto his long-lost soulmate in Bobby.

Dave is, according to his own reports, a somewhat nervous

and ineffectual pedophile. He seemed to have mostly confined himself to furtive fondling of sleeping boys he manages to come in contact with, terrified of being caught. He described himself repeatedly as paranoid to Bobby. (He was a volunteer Big Brother, although an FBI investigation after his arrest found no evidence that "anything inappropriate happened" with any of his charges.) To Bobby, he confesses his frustration at not being able to get anywhere with various young prospects and his anxiety about not knowing how to make the right moves. Dave makes an enthusiastic and appreciative audience for Bobby's vague accounts of his own multiple successes in the kiddie-sex arena, which he dangled before the hapless Dave like a calculated lure.

Bobby's descriptions of his professional life are also becoming more elaborate: he tells a convoluted tale of freelancing for a mafioso-type pornographer and tough guy named Roberto ("He's not a real nice guy when he gets nasty," Bobby warns), spending his time traveling around California doing various photo layouts for this Roberto, including, he informs Dave leadingly, many featuring the elusive object, young boys. As a gesture of trust, Bobby sends Dave some photos of boys through the mail and does some enlargements for Dave of photos of boys Dave sends him (which also allowed San Jose police to trace Dave's fingerprints and identify him as Dean Lambey).

Bobby's professional endeavors and tales of various pornographic escapades inspire no small amount of envy in Dave, as do Bobby's reports of his sexual conquests. "I gotta be doing something wrong," Dave keeps moaning. Dave casts Bobby in the role of pedophilic mentor, frequently requesting advice about how to approach boys successfully, what to do with them once he's made contact, and even shyly solicits basic sexual information such as at what age boys start having erections and orgasms. For a purported pedophile, he's surprisingly uninformed about male sexual development, and he's so out of the loop he can't

even find a kid to cut his overgrown lawn—"a perfectly legitimate situation," as he laments. His self-description as all-round
loser apparently matched his social demeanor: Daniel DePew
described him as a "drip." Indeed, psychological theories of
pedophilic personalities often focus on their inappropriate social
behavior: isolated, sexually inhibited, anxious, and timid, these
men tend to be sexually and emotionally insecure in interactions
with adults. Expecting nothing but rejection and failure there,
beset by feelings of inadequacy, they turn instead to relations
with inappropriate partners such as children.

Dave's timorousness and reassurance seeking alternates
with a second persona, however, one of braggadocio and kinky
fantasy. "I have no morals," he boasts to Bobby early on. "How
kinky would you like to get???" It's this second personality that
Bobby cultivates, and Dave is pathetically grateful to have a new
friend to share his fantasies with. ("Knowing you are on the
bulletin board, I've pretty much gotten into the habit of check-
ing in every day!! Look forward to hearing from you soon!!" he
gushes.) With Bobby's encouragement, Dave allows his fantasies to intensify, and between the two of them, this begins to
evolve into a plan to produce a video, in which a young boy will
somehow be obtained, possibly from a source Dave claims to
have in Florida, and made the unwilling star in a child porn
movie. (At the time, Officer Rodrigues related to the local FBI
that he thought Dave's Florida connection was fictitious.)

At the same time, Dave's uncertainty continues to manifest itself in almost every other line: "Of course by now you
probably think that I'm a real nut case, but what the hey, at least
I'm honest, right?" "I could be game if you are." "Maybe I'm
speaking out of turn, I don't know where your head is about real
heavy stuff . . ." "You probably think I'm a real mental case," he
writes nervously, when Bobby doesn't immediately enthuse over

some particular fantasy element. As long as Bobby keeps reassuring him however, Dave remains a willing player.

Soon this fantasy, or plan ("fantasy" is the term Ashley uses most), is being alluded to regularly, as is the very gruesome possibility that the boy will have to be somehow "disposed of" once the film is wrapped. The necessity of this particular finale is, initially, for Dave and Bobby's self-protection. The conversations move from the bulletin board to lengthy, rambling phone conversations. Following the first phone conversation, Bobby writes to Dave on the bulletin board, "I've been thinking about our conversation and FANTASIZING. I'm leaning toward doing it. I hope you are for real and not pulling my chain. I've done a lot of thinking and find it stimulating." The discussions continue. The idea of somehow getting rid of the boy hangs there, although Dave is never entirely happy about it. While in his braggadocio persona he seems to accept it, but the rest of the time it makes him quite squeamish: he imagines himself growing fond of this imaginary boy, he speaks of him romantically. He refers repeatedly to having moral qualms, but is also willing to discuss possible methods—which he prefers be painless, like a drug overdose. He doesn't want to be present at the end, yet also worries that he could become addicted to killing as a sexual activity. And what if the actual event proves less satisfying than the fantasy? he frets.

Is this a fantasy or a plan? Are these two plotting a crime, or collaboratively spinning out a perverse piece of fiction? Dave seems content to talk endlessly on the phone long-distance, mulling over details and scenarios, debating about how to obtain the boy (kidnap or purchase), what to do with him once they have him (various sexual activities), and what to do with him once they've finished (sell him in South America, give him a drug overdose, return him . . .). It's Bobby who moves these vagaries

closer to reality by telling Dave that boss Roberto will bankroll
the film, discussing marketing, and even dangling before Dave
(who continually complains about money) future projects and
business ventures the two can undertake as buddies.

Dave's reports of his mostly unsatisfactory sexual experiences with boys seem to have been confined, to date, to fondling and a few episodes of oral sex; he's intrigued but also put
off by sadomasochistic possibilities and seems repelled by anal
sex. Reading through over five hundred pages of FBI transcripts
of these conversations one begins to wonder if they were simply a way for Dave to be able to talk about sex (which he seems
not to have much experience at) with Bobby. Of course, the two
of them never, in all these many hours on the phone, refer to
sex with each other: it's never even raised as a possibility. Sex is
always discussed through the intermediary of the abducted child:
perhaps it was the figure of this fictional child that allowed Dave
to sustain this lengthy relationship with an adult. Detective
Bobby, in the interests of entrapping Dave, feigns acceptance,
provides sympathetic, nonjudgmental fraternity, even intimacy.
Dave, in need of a competent therapist if ever anyone was,
responds by casting Bobby to play the role, spontaneously laps-
ing into free-associational speech, alternating between rambling
fantasy, free-form confession, and requests for advice and reassurance. Context is everything: had Dave verbalized his fantasies in a shrink's office at $150 an hour instead of to an
undercover cop, it would have been called therapy. It was a category error that earned him a thirty-year prison term.

In fact, the relationship was carefully engineered to elicit
Dave's intimacies: Rodrigues held regular phone conferences
with the Behavioral Sciences Unit at FBI headquarters in Washington, who advised him on how to play Dave most effectively
and win his trust. (Presumably, the state's nontherapeutic position in pursuing this entrapment case so relentlessly was that

this sort of friendship would have been the catalyst that drove this nervous fondler over the edge into violence and murder. Which, of course, he'd shown no inclination toward previously.) The question of whether Dave was serious or merely fantasizing was immediately raised in Rodrigues's meetings with local FBI agents; their advice was to set up a meeting with Dave as soon as possible to gauge his seriousness. (The FBI behavior experts in Washington were puzzled about why Lambey was so incautious in his conversations with Bobby, having only met him on a bulletin board. Perhaps it's because he never thought it was serious.)

Following the FBI's instructions, after two months of contact, Bobby starts pushing the question of whether Dave *is* serious by repeatedly mentioning the possibility of flying out to the East Coast. "But I don't wanna come out there for nothing, I wanna make sure you're, if we're gonna do it, we're gonna do it." Dave says yes, he's ready to do it. Bobby is at this point initiating all contact with Dave, phoning him frequently, pursuing him like an eager suitor. Bobby now broaches the possibility of bringing a friend in on the plan. The friend, he says, thinks there's a market for these kind of films, and says he's been asking around for buyers for certain "materials" and has possibly found someone interested. *Now Bobby wants Dave to find someone on the East Coast to join in the plan.* Dave argues with him, but Bobby returns to this element again and again. The reason for his insistence is clear. For Bobby and Dave, talking over these lurid possibilities is, legally speaking, just talk, because legally, you can't form a conspiracy with the police. In order for there to be a crime, short of an actual kidnapping (or other than a minor charge for the photos Dave sent through the mail), that is, in order for there to be a criminal conspiracy, there had to be a second person who was not a policeman involved. Bobby's plan is to bring his friend R.J. (actually his undercover partner) in on the plan, and he again encourages Dave to find someone in his area. Or as Bobby puts it, "Let's put the machine in gear and get going."

Soon it develops that the fictional Roberto is sending Bobby and pal R.J. to the East Coast to do a shoot. The two long-distance phone pals can finally meet up. Shortly before this planned meeting Dave seems to drop from sight. "Hey dude, are you around or what?" Bobby writes. "I've been paging you and calling you at home . . . we need to talk to confirm our plans." He even tries fruitlessly to contact Dave on another bulletin board called Harbor Bytes. "Hey dude, are you still on the planet earth or what? I've been trying to get a hold of you but no success. Get hold of me at home." When they finally do connect, Bobby makes it clear to Dave that once in D.C., he won't be able to leave his hotel room. He's on call for Roberto, he says, so the meeting will have to take place at his hotel. Dave doesn't like this at all. His paranoia reasserts itself and he's worried about the room being bugged. Bobby however, reassures him, and Dave finally relaxes. (In fact, the detectives wore body mikes, which made their conversation frequently incomprehensible on the tapes.)

Around this time, one Wednesday night, Daniel DePew logged on to another computer bulletin board called "Drummer," run by an S&M oriented gay porn magazine of the same name. Wednesday was the night DePew usually reserved for himself, spending it apart from his live-in lover, Patrick. His work situation had been frantic the last few months: the company he worked for was about to undergo a takeover, employees had been let go and not replaced, his workload was up, and he was under a lot of stress. (Ironically, or so it would later seem, the company he worked for had numerous government contracts to manufacture wiretap equipment for various national security agencies.) Logging on to one of the gay bulletin boards was a way he relaxed.

The Drummer board allowed a user, once logged on, to have a simultaneous conversation with anyone else logged on at the same time—to chat in person, so to speak. DePew had posted a description of himself and his sexual preferences on the board, indicating a number of very specific activities he liked, all having to do with dominance and submission. He advertised himself as a "top," that is, the dominant partner, or master. Dean Lambey also had a description on the board, advertising himself as being into father-son type relationships, as well as infantilism. Lambey (calling himself Ashley again) saw DePew's ad, saw he was on line, and beeped him, requesting a conversation. The two conversed (in writing) for a bit, and Ashley asked for DePew's home phone number; DePew gave him his work number.

Ashley called a few days later and eagerly suggested getting together. DePew proposed they meet in a bar, which was his practice when meeting someone he didn't know. In case they didn't hit it off he could down a few drinks and make a quick escape. Ashley, though, was adamant about meeting in a hotel, so they made a date to meet at the Radisson in Alexandria, near where DePew lived, but at least two hours from Ashley's home in Richmond.

It wasn't uncommon for DePew to meet someone with mutual sexual interests over a bulletin board and get together to have sex. In the world of gay S&M, a good top is hard to find (everyone wants to be dominated, it seems), and DePew was sometimes contacted through referral by people who wanted his services. He'd made the switch to top himself a few years before, partly, he says, because the tops he encountered were so terrible at it: abusive rather than caring, or dangerous. (In his first encounter with rough sex, he'd cracked a rib.) Also he was getting older, had a hairy chest, and didn't want to shave his beard, so he more or less grew into the role. But he still considered himself primarily a bottom, at least psychologically (he says that when he fantasizes it's as a bottom), and yearned for someone else to take control, for a man he could look up to.

DePew was a man who'd always felt like a failure at masculinity. In a conversation with him, almost every question circles back to the problem of manhood. Masculinity looms, grail-like, as something quite unattainable, yet something incredibly important, and this overriding sense of masculine failure fueled the most pervasive feelings of insufficiency and inferiority. He'd known he was gay from an early age and never made any attempt to conceal it; in rural Maryland in the seventies where he grew up, that was a particularly daunting experience. His father frequently berated him for not being enough of a man and refused to talk to him for several years after Dan acknowledged he was gay.

His father's rejection was rounded out by his general social ostracization. From an early age he yearned to be one of the guys—it was all he wanted in life. But he never had any social success, except as "the brain," and was exiled from sports and other masculine spheres. So of course what he most craved was masculine camaraderie and approval; his solution was to give all the boys in the neighborhood blow jobs, which they accepted, then pretended hadn't happened. After a fairly indifferent turn at being a father, Daniel DePew, Sr.—a second- or third-generation alcoholic who worked as a sanitation engineer in a sewage treatment plant—moved out, divorcing Dan's mother, Barbara, a mail carrier. This was when he was twelve. It was also at age twelve that he started having sex. His overwhelmingly negative feelings about his father seem to stem both from bitterness at not having had much of a father-son relationship, but also because he regards his father as not having been particularly successful at masculinity either. He told psychiatrists who compiled a postarrest psychological profile that he'd actually had quite a close relationship with his father when he was younger but that his father's alcoholism put a stop to this, which suggests that at one time he did have the masculine attention he craved, and it was abruptly withdrawn.

The specter of that paternal absence seemed to hover throughout his adult life, reappearing continually in the shape of a pressing sexual desire. His first entrée into S&M subculture came when he took over the job of bootblack boy at a local leather bar. He describes in elaborate detail the procedure of polishing men's boots: the man sat in "a great big chair" while Dan, perched below, went through an elaborate routine of putting the wax on with his bare hands, working it in, buffing it with his bare hands (he says he'd have blisters when he got home). I asked what he liked about that. "He's sitting up there," he replied, "and I'm down here and I'm doing this for him and he's looking down at me. . . . That's where it started—the worshiping-type role." "What were you worshiping?" I asked. "The man," he said. "A man. This masculine, virile, everything I wanted to be type man." "And felt you weren't?" "Everything I felt I wasn't," he confirmed, reprising the now-familiar theme of masculine insufficiency. But when he described the worshipful intimacy of the relationship of "bootblack" to "man," his description centered most vividly around the moment of looking up into the man's eyes, from the position of squatting at his feet. That is, from the position of a child looking up into the parent's eyes. The payoff of making himself into a menial, a bootblack, seems to have been contained in that glance, one that he recounts vividly and sentimentally, in which his adoring, worshiping look at the man above him is returned. And it seemed to me that it was simply a child's desire for love that he was describing and living out in that moment, and the devastating absence of that in his own life that induced him to read love into a moment that for anyone else would have been simply a shoeshine. His lifelong quest had been to recreate such moments at any cost, and his ability to so misread a situation, or to so creatively transform it—to find the love he was looking for in all the wrong places— would, in the end, destroy his life.

Dan's first experience with someone he thought of as sufficiently masculine was an early sex partner named Donny, when he was about fourteen. The experience with Donny left an irrevocable mark, jarring and somehow realigning something within his emotional circuitry. Donny, although not in any self-conscious way into sadomasochism, was terrifically rough. Dan describes Donny picking him up and hurling him across the room, and Dan seemed to think he'd finally been let in on the masculine roughhousing he'd always missed out on. (He described this as a "boys will be boys kind of thing" with a kind of pride.) Always hyperattentive to the question of whether he was being treated as masculine or not, Dan was in rapture. For him, Donny's roughness was not only a sign of Donny's masculinity, but more important, a chance to prove his own masculinity by being tough enough to "take it." (His own father never disciplined him, and he recounts this as another paternal failure. It's as if he thinks he'd missed out on some masculinity-building experience.) His description of having anal sex for the first time with Donny, which, as he describes it (painful, unlubricated) sounds like an almost rapelike experience, turns into an ode to masculinity: "It was so natural, so masculine for Donny to just take it the way he wanted it."

Dan's experience with Donny wasn't that Donny was in the "masculine role" and Dan in the "feminine," it was that they were both masculine because Donny was rough like a man, and Dan was "taking it like a man." It started to become clear to me while hearing this story, and noting the nostalgia with which it was recalled, that DePew's ardent dedication to violence stemmed in large part from its stereotypical association with masculinity. Lacking, as he puts it, "masculine role models," he was picking and sifting through the culture, searching for behaviors and attitudes to adopt, and settling on those that the culture itself had already stamped with the imprimatur of maleness: he seems to have gotten a lot of input from cowboy movies particularly, and mentions John Wayne fondly.

Had some core sense of masculinity been more securely implanted within him, this quest would hardly have been necessary; neither, one suspects, would his devotion to sadomasochistic sex and fantasy. As a bottom, it could feel fantastic to have a loving daddy, ". . . you know, warm, loving, and he's in charge, and Daddy will take care of it. If there's any problem Daddy will handle it, if you're upset you can go to Daddy. . . ." Later on, as a top, he took extraordinary pride in being the kind of good father he himself never had: ushering his "boys," as he called his bottoms, into manhood. "Raising them," as he puts it. He describes teaching his lover Patrick (also the product of an indifferent father) how to rebuild an engine, change the oil in the car, how to use tools. ("I'd ask him to give me that nine-millimeter wrench over there and he walks out with a pair of vice grips," he recalled, with what can only be described as paternal affection.) "Where did *you* learn to use tools?" I asked. "From a book called *Motor Manual*," he answered, an autodidact of masculinity. His devotion to tools and auto repair are, of course, again part of the official repertoire of masculine stereotypes. But in both his sexual roles, bottom and top, he was also unremittingly devoted to repair: repairing, then reliving, in idealized and sexualized fashion, these coveted paternal moments.

His formal entrée into the world of S&M actually began when he started frequenting leather bars in an attempt to rid himself of the feminine mannerisms he'd picked up in the local gay bar while serving in the air force in Biloxi, Mississippi. The air force was his first experience away from home, his first experience of gay social life. To fit in he'd refashioned himself into a southern queen, and becoming a southern queen meant, first of all, becoming bulimic: "I would not eat. If I ate anything I immediately went and threw it up, unless I was depressed and then I binge ate, and then I felt guilty, and *then* I went and threw it up." His goal was to obtain a twenty-eight-inch waist, he said.

Suddenly we were girlfriends: his mannerisms became much more broadly feminine than they'd been—he was animated, and his voice even seemed higher. "But I found I had thirty-two-inch hipbones so a twenty-eight-inch waist is impossible. I had to get rid of all my clothes, I had to go out and buy these silk things with drapey sleeves, and big flowing things, and I started doing my nails—I always bit my nails before but now I was polishing them. I was an extremely unhappy person. I hated everything about this—doing my nails, and my hair, and not eating, and I was always so fat, I could not lose *enough* weight. And up until then I hadn't had any chest hair, then I was getting all this chest hair, and that was disgusting, I had to shave it all off. I can't look my best, because I'm becoming this ape. . . . And so I'm going through all this, and I *don't* have a lover, I can't get one. . . . Of course now I look back on it: Who would want to go home with something that was all bony like that?"

I had to explain that the reason I was laughing was that his description of becoming a southern queen was so close to the day-to-day experience of being gendered female in this culture (at least it's mine): fanatically consumed with dieting, depilation, and clothes. His makeshift approach to adopting femininity was like his selective adoption of masculinity: it was the stereotypical extremes he was most drawn to, which, in effect, meant their respective pathologies. For the male role, it was masculinity's pathological proximity to violence that he seized on; for the feminine, its debilitating anxieties and fixation on appearance. It was either going to be Rambo or Blanche DuBois. Gender, for DePew, was a sort of playacting. What seemed lacking was something felt or internal that would supply, in some automatic, unstudied way, information on how to act, feel, and live a particular gender identity in a way that felt "natural." Absent that, the predefined roles of S&M offered a replacement, in addition to the opportunity to keep reliving and repeating the problematic father-son relationship.

Once Dan was entrenched in the social world of S&M, sex was organized through fantasy and role-playing. Consequently, when he met up with "Dave Ashley" at the Radisson, discussing fantasies was the first order of business. Ashley had rented a room, but DePew, who had been hoping the assignation would lead to sex, found Ashley repellent and was turned off. DePew, who's a nice-looking guy, describes Ashley as "a troll," with an oily complexion, unclean hair—totally unappealing in every way. Ashley immediately brought up his interest in children. DePew says he told him that he wasn't into kiddie sex but said, "I can be open-minded." Ashley described the kidnapping–snuff film scenario as a favored fantasy and mentioned his pornographer friends from California. DePew, a crime magazine buff, critiqued the plan; getting into it, he gave Ashley tips on how to dispose of the body to make it unidentifiable.

In DePew's creed about being a top, the first thing you do with someone you don't know is discuss fantasies. It's a way of getting to know someone, and of building up the necessary trust to have a sexual encounter in which one person makes himself completely vulnerable to the other. DePew has quite an elaborate set of theories about being a top, an earnestness about the responsibility involved—part of his didactic dedication to the good father role. Trust, caring, sensitivity are essential elements. He explains, "It's customary that you sit and you talk and you get to know the person, because in an S&M situation, it's important to develop a rapport with your bottom so that you know where his head is at, you know not to go too far. Going too far doesn't necessarily mean that you hurt the person," he explains. "You can go too far and scare them, and so then you have to put their head space back together and you've got to reassure them that they're a good person, that they're somebody to be respected."

DePew says that he had no idea whether Ashley was serious, or a "standard flake" who just got off on talking that way, but that kidnapping fantasies, arrest fantasies, prisoner-of-war fantasies, even execution fantasies were fairly standard in his social circles. DePew and Ashley spent about an hour and a half talking, didn't have sex, and parted. DePew says he didn't expect or want to be in contact with Ashley again. Three weeks later Ashley left a message on DePew's answering machine telling him that his friends from California were in town and that he'd like the four of them to get together. Ashley had described DePew to Bobby, suggesting him as a possible addition to the snuff film scenario (complying with Bobby's command to come up with a fourth person on the East Coast). Without DePew's being aware of it, his name had been mentioned more and more frequently as a part of the plot, in the role of executioner in the snuff film. Now the two detective-pornographers, Bobby and R.J., had indeed flown to the East Coast and, apparently taking no chances, had booked into a Sheraton hotel around the corner from Ashley's home in Richmond, rather than staying in D.C.

Calling Ashley to arrange a meeting, they tried unsuccessfully to get him to contact DePew and persuade DePew to join them. To Ashley was left the task of explaining the realities of

D.C. rush hour traffic to the two Californians—that it would take three or four hours for Dan to get down to Richmond from Washington on a Friday night. Dave does try to call Dan but only has his work number, doesn't reach him, and doesn't leave a number for Dan to call him back.

The meeting with Ashley and the detectives starts out like an awkward blind date, with lengthy discussions of the weather, then cars, then the merits of various California cities as compared to those on the East Coast. Bobby's partner, R.J., who is playing the role of tough guy, finally gets down to business by telling Dave that they have "basically the same kind of interests" and pulling out a bound book of sadomasochistic pornography. R.J. asks Dave if he has any pornography with him, and this segues into a discussion of the snuff film plot.

Throughout the conversation, Ashley raises numerous objections to both the kidnapping scenario and the snuff scenario; each time he does, the two detectives lead him like a horse on a tight rein, back to the booty. Ashley broaches the possibility of obtaining a boy from his Florida contact, but it will take maybe a month, and R.J. protests vehemently, "Man, I thought that's why we came out here. I didn't want to wait no fucking month"; thus back to the kidnapping option. (This is the Florida connection that Officer Rodrigues had previously told the FBI he thought was fictional.) They discuss the possibility of DePew doing the snuff and Ashley says of the boy, "Ideally I'd just like to, you know, kick it out. But you can't kick it out." R.J. says, "Let it walk?" Dave says, "Yeah." R.J. says, "Then let it talk." Dave agrees, but later repeats, "You know, the ending is not my particular favorite part, I got to tell you that. If there was some way we could do what we wanted without the ending, I think we'd probably do that." He rues again, "You know, fantasies don't

29

always turn out the way you think they will." Bobby reassures him, "Sometimes they do though," and Dave agrees that sometimes they're even better, but worries that if the boy is screaming and crying, he won't enjoy it at all.

The main purpose of this meeting seems to be to get Ashley to commit to the plan and to commit to getting DePew in on the plan also. In other words, the detectives have flown from California to Richmond *in order to engineer a crime that wouldn't occur without their instigation*. Within the space of two hours, R.J. and Bobby repeat seventeen times their desire to meet with DePew. R.J.: "Have you talked to Dan about this?" "I'd sure like to meet this guy. . . ." "I want to make sure I have a face-to-face with this man. . . ." "I think we should include Dan." "I think we still need to meet him just because he knows." "Will Dan help on that?" "What's Dan's ideas about it?" Bobby: "[I want to] meet up with Dan, see where he's coming from, you know. I think we really should." R.J. seizes on the point that because Ashley has mentioned the plan to DePew, DePew *has* to be in on it, or at least R.J. has to meet him to reassure himself that Dan is trustworthy. Dave tries telling R.J. that Dan has only a vague notion of the plan, and R.J. barks, "Don't be fucking stroking me along here. Does he know what we're doing? Yes or no?" Toward the end of the meeting R.J. states, "I guess we're in agreement, Dan's going to do it?" Dave: "Well, I mean we—I don't think we can—" Bobby: "If he's interested." Dave: "We can say that now until you talk to him because he might not—you know, what if you talk to him and you're not comfortable, well, then that changes things altogether." Dave tried to suggest again that they don't need another guy, even one person could pull it off, he insists. R.J. is adamant that they need four.

At this point, Bobby had been courting Ashley for close to four months. Without another person involved, there was no crime. And if there was no crime, these were four wasted months, and a lot of wasted law enforcement dollars as well. The meter was ticking.

On parting, R.J. instructs Dave, "See if you can't get a hold of Dan tonight or first thing in the morning. . . . I definitely want to talk to him on a face-to-face." He repeats this twice. Ashley reiterates his qualms, "But I'm just not sure I want to actually do the deed, cause I have some morals, you know." But he follows with, "Then again, I may really enjoy doing the deed, I don't know." Ashley's commitment to the plan seems not entirely intact at this point. Without the two detectives stringing him along, would he have continued his involvement, which never did go beyond talk? If either Bobby or R.J. had agreed that this scheme probably wasn't the greatest idea, would Dave perhaps have been grateful? But of course the purpose of their trip east was to ensure that there *was* a crime, not give Ashley an out. Ashley gave them Dan DePew's work number before he left.

When Dan DePew and Dave Ashley had their unsatisfying assignation in Alexandria, Dan had suggested that his role in the fantasized film would be as the executioner: he would do the snuff. What does killing a child mean to you? I asked him. Oddly, DePew answered as though I had asked him, Who *is* the child? (In fact, there never was any particular child targeted or even identified as a prospective victim, one of the more questionable aspects of this case.) He first answered, "Remember that when you say 'child' it depends on what's going through the mind of the speaker. I wasn't visualizing some nine-year-old choirboy—more along the lines of some sixteen-year-old street punk doing drive-by shootings." Then he added, "Maybe like the kind of kid I was terrorized by when I was younger."

In further discussions, DePew's answer to this question went through a number of oscillations, quite reminiscent of those

31

Freud describes in his 1919 paper "A Child Is Being Beaten," which opens with the odd report that during the course of psychoanalysis, patients frequently confessed to having an identical, recurrent, strangely pleasurable yet guilty fantasy that begins "A child is being beaten." The paper is based on the close study of six cases (reportedly including Freud's daughter Anna). According to Freud there were numerous others. "Who was the child that was being beaten?" he wonders. "Who was it who is beating the child?" Answers are initially elusive. "Nothing could be ascertained that threw any light upon all these questions— only the timid reply: 'I know nothing more about it: a child is being beaten.'"[9]

In exploring this fantasy with patients, Freud found that the fantasy went through three distinct incarnations. In the initial version ("A child is being beaten"), the child being beaten isn't the one producing the fantasy, and the child producing the fantasy isn't doing the beating either. As this is discussed further, a second version of the fantasy emerges, in which the person doing the beating is identified as the child's father. This is a more unconscious moment that is summed up as "My father is beating the child" and is further amplified as "My father is beating the child whom I hate." In analyzing this second stage of the fantasy, it emerges that the child who is being beaten has now changed into the child who is producing the fantasy: "I am being beaten by my father." This version of the fantasy is accompanied by a high degree of sexual pleasure, says Freud. In the third stage of the fantasy, the person doing the beating is no longer the father, but some other authority figure who is the father's representative, and the child being beaten is no longer the one producing the fantasy. Here the fantasizer's role is that of an onlooker, joined by a number of other children looking on.

In Freud's interpretation, the origins of the fantasy are actually pretty mundane, not so very different from the origin of so much general everyday unhappiness and neurosis. He traces the early stages of the fantasy to feelings of childhood abandonment, which often come with the birth of a sibling. The notion of the father beating another child signifies "My father does not love this other child, he loves only me." In the second stage, guilt intervenes, and the earlier sadistic fantasy ("He loves only me, not the other child, for he is beating it") turns masochistic ("I am being beaten by my father"). (The guilt is also an expression of guilty sexual love for the father.) In the third form of the fantasy, in which the person producing the fantasy is a spectator and the person doing the beating is the father's representative, Freud sees these as simply masked versions of the father and child and interprets it as "My father is beating the other child, he loves only me."

When I asked Dan, "What does killing a child mean to you?" and he answered with the description of his sixteen-year-old tormentor, I said, "So it's a kind of revenge fantasy?" He answered, "When you have a ninety-eight-pound weakling and you have sand kicked in your face and now you're thinking of revenge, you're going to imagine something a lot worse than kicking sand in Mr. Macho's face."

This figure of himself as a tormented and terrorized ninety-eight-pound weakling is one he returned to frequently as a source of his buried anger and resentment. (In reality he's over six feet tall and weighs maybe one hundred and ninety pounds.) "The driver that cut me off, the big guy who treated me like a ninety-eight-pound weakling, all of those situations where I should have been man enough to not have it happen to me, to be walked all over and treated like a nebbish, all of that aggression has been internalized because I'm not man enough to bring it out." The charge of not being man enough was, of course, his father's accusation to him. And invariably, whenever he discusses this snuff film scenario, and when he describes the fictional child to be "snuffed," what he describes instead is a rivalry between himself (the ninety-eight-pound weakling) and a macho tormentor. This tormentor appears in various guises: the sixteen-year-old street punk, the boss, the driver who cuts him off—but all are versions of a superior masculine figure, one who reveals to him his own deficient masculinity. The child he wants to kill (not a nine-year-old choirboy but a sixteen-year-old street punk) seems to be the rival for his father's affections: the boy who *is* man enough, the son his father wanted, instead of the "ninety-eight-pound weakling" he got.

At another moment, when I asked him about his anger at this imaginary boy, he answered: "The anger? It's more at myself, because the ninety-eight-pound weakling only gets walked on because he lets somebody walk on him—letting the waiter give you bad service because you're too afraid to speak up, letting your boss walk all over you because you can't take a stand—and I was always well known for being able to work with the most difficult bosses because I'm going to swallow it all." When I asked him whom he would identify with in the snuff film scenario he said with the kid, because he invariably identifies with the bottom in any scene, even though in his life he had made the switch to the top, to the father role. His life as a sadomasochist afforded the opportunity to move between all of the different positions of the beating fantasy: the child being beaten (the bottom, "the boy"), the father doing the beating (the top, "the daddy"), the onlooker, and even as the snuff film executioner, the vanquisher of the rival for his father's affections.

There's an eerie line in Freud's paper that reads: "People who harbor phantasies of this kind develop a special sensitiveness and irritability towards anyone whom they can put among the class of fathers. They allow themselves to be easily offended by a person of this kind, and in that way (to their own sorrow and cost) bring about the realization of the imagined situation of being beaten by their father." Rereading the essay, I thought immediately of the imprisoned DePew—particularly when Freud remarks of the third phase of the beating fantasy that "the person beating is a substitute from the class of fathers." What else is the state's role in the DePew case, but the foremost father in the class of fathers, which in clapping DePew in prison for thirty-three years neatly brought about "the realization of the imagined situation of being beaten by the father." I had asked DePew, although I felt quite like a sadist in doing so, if he thought it was at all ironic that so much of his fantasy life revolved around scenarios of punishment and that now he found himself spending his life in prison. Had he, at any level, wanted to be punished? (I think, in posing this question, that I must have intuited that I was talking with a person incapable of expressing anger.) He merely answered ruefully that his arrest fantasies had turned out to be nothing like the reality.

When Bobby called Daniel DePew (out of the blue, as far as Dan was concerned), he left a message on DePew's voice mail at work identifying himself as a friend of Dave Ashley's. He said that he hadn't heard from Ashley, was worried, and asked Dan to call him back. He also said, knowingly dangling just the right carrot, that they had "mutual interests" he wanted to chat about. Dan left a message for Bobby that he didn't have Ashley's phone number (which he didn't) but would leave a message for him to call Bobby on the computer bulletin board (which he did). The next day Bobby left another message for Dan: he was on his way to the East Coast and hoped they could get together. (This was the agents' second trip east.) When they finally spoke, Bobby invited Dan to come out to his hotel and have dinner. Apparently not trusting Ashley to deliver Dan, the cops baited a hook and reeled him into the setup themselves. Dan, who never stopped questing for the perfect scene, for that one perfect man, wasn't about to turn down the invitation.

When Dan got to the hotel, he was surprised to find that Bobby wasn't alone. R.J. was there with him. They discuss traffic, awkwardly. Bobby fixes Dan a drink while R.J. tells him they're concerned because they haven't heard from Ashley. Dan explains that he doesn't really know anything about Ashley other than his name, doesn't have his phone number, and has only met him once, via the computer bulletin board. Dan turns the conversation to computers, which leads to a discussion of air travel, air crashes, the Eastern Airlines strike; Bobby then suggests they order dinner from room service. Dan, wondering just what kind of situation he's found himself in, notes that they don't even want to leave the room to have dinner and takes this as a hopeful sign that some kind of scene is in the works. He begins talking aimlessly about his job and manages to get in quite a lengthy description of his day-to-day routine before R.J. interjects, "When was the last time that you tried to call David? How long have you known him?" then peppers Dan with a series of questions about what Ashley's told him about them.

Dan's not particularly interested in talking about Ashley. He explains that he lives with his lover Patrick, an artist, that he usually spends Wednesday nights alone—R.J. turns the conversation back to Ashley and their previous visit to D.C. three weeks earlier, when Ashley had told them about Dan. Dan repeats that he and Ashley had met only once. R.J. obliquely introduces the snuff film scheme: "We were just, you know, uh . . . What is the word I'm searching for? Sensitive?" Bobby: "No. That's not—" Dan interjects, "Highly illegal?" confirming that he does know about the plan. R.J. says, "That too, yeah." They all laugh. R.J. continues, "We were real curious as to what he had said about us." Bobby adds, "The thing R.J. is trying to say is that we wanna see where you're coming from."

DePew says now that he thought at the time, at least initially, that they were talking about a scene, a fantasy. It's a common practice in his world for guys to get together in a hotel room, discuss their fantasies, and have sex. Not only that, but when Dan walked into the hotel room, he'd found himself immediately attracted to R.J., who was, of course, playing the role of the heavy. He describes knowing within the first five or ten minutes of meeting someone whether to treat a man as an equal or take the subservient role. There's a sort of subconscious calculation that gets made, and Dan made the instant decision that R.J. was "the man" in the scene. "He had a more dominating personality than I do, my personality is more, I'm not going to say that I'm unpopular, but I never attain instant popularity or instant control of the room or the center of attention. . . . R.J. was definitely, you walk in the room, and spotlights, charisma, fanfare, 'He's here,' that kind of thing." R.J., a cop playing the role of the muscle, must have come across as Dan's conception of flawless masculinity, the kind of guy he's always attracted to, the sixteen-year-old street punk grown up: "The one who's going to steal my car, steal my credit cards, and rob me, I usually end up being attracted to that one," he says ruefully. "The one who has an edge of danger?" I ask. "Yes," he confirms.

In Dan's sense of their respective roles, R.J. was the top and Dan was the second top—that is, bottom to R.J., but top to Bobby. Interestingly, when I spoke to Officer James Rodrigues, who played the role of Bobby, he sketched a similar hierarchical breakdown of who was top in the room. But in his version, DePew was the top, R.J. was second, Ashley was third (he described Ashley as also being quite aggressive), and he, playing the more effeminate role, was the bottom. When I questioned his ranking of DePew as the toughest, he said that DePew had admitted to killing before (which DePew says he'd made up). But then, Bobby and R.J. also claimed to have made snuff films before. The relations in this room must have been like some Pirandello play, with each character performing an illusory role that the others completely believe, with each convinced by the others' roles, but unaware of how convincing they are in their own. (There was also a video camera inside a lamp, adding to the dramaturgy.)

R.J.'s masculine allure not only kept DePew immobilized in the room, it also dictated that he attempt to impress R.J. with his own masculine prowess. To Dan, that meant his capacity for violence. Signaling his aspirations as second top, he described his relationship with Patrick as one in which Dan beats him, hangs him, and gets to take his irritations out on him. He also described an incident when he was stationed in Greece, claiming that he beat up an American backpacker and was on the verge of killing him. (He told me this was a fantasy. There was an American backpacker, but nothing violent happened: he insists he's terrified of real-life violence. Nevertheless, this supposed incident was brought up at DePew's trial as evidence of intent.) So if R.J. wanted Dan to talk about making a snuff film, Dan was only too willing to comply. When R.J. asked him where he was coming from, he replied, continuing the fantasy he'd set up with Ashley, "Well actually, my main interest is in doing the snuff." Having cast R.J. as his "man," his personal code dictated that "when your man tells you to do something you do it, when he tells you to be something, you'd better be it." What he thought he was supposed to be was the henchman in an imaginary snuff film. He told them that he didn't want any part of the kidnapping, but would take care of the ending.

Over the next three hours, whenever R.J. cues him, Dan obediently spins out ever more violent scenarios about his role in the film. And perhaps it wasn't an entirely unexciting prospect to him that it might *not* be only a fantasy—that these could be real tough-guy pornographers who weren't playacting. As long as all he has to do is talk about it. R.J. says things like, "We're very concerned, I mean, we're making trips out here and we just wanna make sure that we're not being set up or you know, spinning our wheels." They tell him they've made snuff films before. Dan, who's being plied with scotch (he says he had six or seven drinks there on top of the two before he'd left home—even the agents comment on how much he's drinking), keeps attempting to turn the conversation to topics other than the snuff film. He's becoming progressively more disjointed, but the detectives keep valiantly turning the conversation back to Ashley. "What kind of agreement did you make with Dave?" R.J. asks. Dan answers, "I made no agreement with Dave. I told him we were talking in a purely hypothetical sense." He says that he never trusted Ashley, and they all talk a lot about not trusting Ashley. The agents are pissed off he's not there. He's neither called nor shown up, and they must have seen their conspiracy slowly wafting away into the ether. R.J. tries to get Dan to call Ashley, and Dan explains that Ashley's at least two hours away in Richmond. R.J. asks if Dan has tried to get a hold of Ashley himself and Dan reminds him he has no way of getting hold of him other than leaving a computer message. Bobby calls Ashley again, and as he's leaving yet another message on the answering machine, R.J. instructs him to say "Dan wants to know where you're at." Bobby instead says, "R.J. wants to know where the hell you're at." R.J. adds, "So does Dan," and Bobby adds, "So does Dan." Dan asks them not to give Ashley his home number, and R.J. assures him that he and Bobby are "very, very discreet."

Ashley finally calls. Bobby and R.J. give him a hard time on the phone about not showing up. Bobby says, "Hold on, Dan wants to talk to you" (which he didn't) and adds, to Dan, "Make him make a commitment." Dan talks to Ashley briefly and hands the phone back to Bobby, who tries the get-tough approach with Ashley. "I think there's some things we gotta sit down and talk about," he says sternly. Ashley grumbles. Bobby protests, "Well, it's not spur-of-the-moment. It's just basically we thought things were discussed with Dan by you in a little bit more specific form as to who the people were that were gonna be involved and stuff." It's clear that the agents are desperately trying to hold this conspiracy together, and trying everything they can to get the four of them together in a room where they can be taped discussing the plot. Without that crucial meeting it seems unlikely that a conspiracy charge would hold up.

The rest of the evening Dan is rambling and drunkenly confessional. What emerges most clearly in the conversation is the way his affinity for tools and home mechanics swerved into his preoccupation with sadomasochism. The result is a passion for sexual gadgetry: his sexual repertoire includes hanging, electrocution, strangling, and other arcane technologies—anything that requires a trip to the hardware store, it seems. He tells them about a bed he built for sadomasochistic scenes, describing in great detail not so much what he does on it, but how he constructed it: the tools, the type of lumber, and the fixtures—down to the last eyehook. He's like a sadomasochistic Mr. Goodwrench. (He complains affectionately, as he will later do to me, about Patrick and tools: "The boy doesn't know a socket wrench from a screwdriver and I have to graphically describe the tool so he knows what to go back to the toolbox to get, and he loses his patience and ends up stripping bolts. . . .") R.J. relates the story of a friend who built a contraption he calls a "rotisserator" for erotic self-electrocution, and ended up putting himself into cardiac arrest. Dan says earnestly, "Well, the thing is to know the flow of the electricity that you're using," explaining that you have to isolate it from standard house current with a transformer. R.J. jokes, "It was a shock to him, too." Dan launches into another how-to on electrical shock below the waist as opposed to above, and where on the body to safely pass current—not through the heart, apparently.

His boy-mechanic side emerges especially vividly when R.J. asks him to discuss various stratagems for the snuff film, and in every case Dan knows just the right tool for the job: to dispose of the body he knows what kind of acid to use to make it unidentifiable, where to buy a roll of sheet plastic to wrap it in— he even knows how much the plastic sells for. (He's also a devotee of *True Detective*–type magazines and is full of obscure and detailed information on crime and detection.) He frequently free-associates to his own youth, his ancedotes about his boyhood verging suddenly into the snuff film plan and the future victim. When he proposes dumping the body in a swamp in southern Maryland near where he grew up, it occasions a description of his teenage initiation into sex; by the end of the evening he's covered most of his adolescence as he flip-flops between the boy victim and himself as a youth. (Who is the child being beaten?) But the detectives are less interested in the past than in the present, and tonight DePew's designated role, egged on by R.J., is to be a criminal Mr. Fix-it. The autodidact's pedagogical zeal was surely DePew's downfall at the trial, where this rhetorical mode was understood as criminal intent, rather than overcompensation for a tenuous purchase on masculinity.

How could he not have any idea that he was being set up? I asked DePew. He suggested, with apologies to my female sensibilities (this amused me), that he was thinking with his dick. I suggested that perhaps he was thinking with his fantasies. Whichever the case, his particular emotional landscape made him the perfect candidate for this entrapment scheme: a tangled relation to issues of authority and manhood left him excessively deferential to and excessively impressed by the two undercover cops playing tough-guy roles as mob-financed pornographers. His lifelong quest for masculine "role models" left him completely unskeptical of them: one suspects that the worse their performances were, and the more they overacted, the better it worked on him. Whether they knew it or not (and they must have), these agents managed to push all his buttons, to yank him around by all his uncertainties. He was too eager to please, and titillated by his fear of them, too fascinated to back off, then finally too authentically fearful. They said vague threatening-sounding things about taking steps to protect their interests; he says he worried that if he tried to back out they'd kill him, or kill Patrick.

When did it stop being a turn-on to be afraid? I asked. When did it become real fear? "When it became quite apparent that these guys were very serious about this. Nobody's getting undressed, we're not finally getting personal, the signs aren't escalating where they're supposed to go, this is not turning out to be the prelude to a scene." So why did he stay? And why did he return? "Looking back I can only tell you how I felt at the time. I took the only course of action I could come up with." Which was, he says, to play along, to not piss them off. He felt he didn't have any alternatives: had he actually gone to the police it would have been his word against theirs. (He was also terrified that a scandal would endanger his government security clearance. Without it he'd be unemployable in the D.C. area, and being gay already kept him at a low level.) And this is a man terrified of dealing with authority in general, whether cops or mobsters. "Men frighten me," he said. I asked why. "They don't all have my internal governor, they can be violent and cruel for the sake of being violent and cruel, so that it hurts and it doesn't feel like it does during a scene." (An "internal governor" is another *Popular Mechanics*–type device.) By way of self-protection he told them a technically complicated story about having stored the vital details about them and their plan on his work computer, which would automatically dump to paper if anything happened to him and someone else tried to open his files. He also saved their phone messages on his office voice-mail system.

Of course, he now berates himself for not having had the courage to stand up to them—it's another failure of masculinity. At one point he described to the agents what kind of men make the best bottom. It's gay men who have spent their lives hating themselves and are consequently "the most submissive and the best bottoms because they hate themselves so much, they want you to do everything you can do to them . . . they're such dirty filthy people, it's like they're paying their penance." It seems likely that he was describing himself. So like a good bottom, he agreed to come back in two days and meet with the detectives again, and with the elusive Dave Ashley.

At the second meeting Ashley shows up first. He's oddly belligerent and immediately begins sparring with R.J., issuing various complaints about what he claims has been their cavalier treatment of him. He tells the two agents they're just like bitchy old women. "Bitch, bitch, bitch," he says repeatedly. "It must be the damn smog out there [in California] in the air that goes to your brains or something." R.J. asks, "Bring any pictures, by chance?" Ashley says, "Geez, what does this guy think I am?" R.J. takes a tough stance. "What do I think you are? I think you're the guy that stood us up night before last. That's what I think." R.J. tells Ashley that when he hadn't shown up, he'd thought Ashley was setting them up. (The technique of the undercover cop seems to be to frequently accuse the people you're setting up of trying to set you up; apparently this is meant to deflect their suspicions of you.) Dave replies, logically, "See, I would

think just the opposite. How would I set you up if I didn't show?"
Ashley's not in a cooperative mood. He tells them he's been too
busy to look around for locations and couldn't get away to meet
them the other day. He doesn't sound entirely happy to be there.
He keeps saying, "Bitch, bitch, bitch," whenever anyone says
anything to him.

DePew arrives and immediately requests a drink. He's
nervous. Bobby had called during the day to make sure he
showed up. There's aimless conversation about water fluorida-
tion and other equally pressing topics, until R.J. puts things on
track. "We were just talking about our venture here," he tells
Dan. The four settle in to discuss possible locations for the filming, although a location was never ultimately agreed on. They
also never agreed on whether to kidnap a child or not, or whether
to buy or rent a car. None of the plans were ever finalized. The
more DePew drinks, the more he seems, again, to spontaneously
relate the snuff scenario to his own youth.

But DePew's primary role, as in the previous meeting, is
to offer lengthy expertise on any technical or mechanical topic.
Of course, he's indefatigable on anything automotive—which
extends metonymically to roads, driver's licenses, and anything
connected to the DMV (how to obtain multiple out-of-state
driver's licenses so as not to have to pay speeding tickets, how
to get new Social Security numbers to get new driver's licenses,
how to forge a power of attorney to transfer title of your car to
someone else to get out of tickets, even the best time of day to
go to the DMV). What emerges is a certain obsessiveness about
outsmarting government bureaucracies: an antagonism to the
class of fathers, as Freud would put it. (Of course he knows the
best way to cheat on your taxes and claims he can even get his
Social Security contributions repaid to him.) There's something
disquieting about a zeal for mastery so acute, yet so oblivious:
at the same time he's explaining to the two undercover agents

just how phone-tap technology works, he's being recorded himself; at the same time he carefully advises the other three on how to evade the tentacles of governmental bureaucracies, he himself is the subject of a massive and concerted multiagency offensive.

DePew is a wealth of information on crime techniques and crime detection: he offers counsel on what kind of clothes to wear when committing a crime; the superiority of chloroform over ether; the superiority of plastic tie wraps (the police use these when making large-scale arrests) over handcuffs and how to configure them most effectively. At another point he cautions the agents to turn on the television so their conversation can't be overheard in the hall. (It was the lamp he should have been worried about.) At various points he does seem to be trying to throw monkey wrenches into their plans: talking at great length about unfeasible options, then shooting them down; insisting they all take part in the snuff when Ashley has repeatedly expressed qualms about it. He told me later that this had been his strategy: appearing to play along, while never intending to go through with it. But every time he opened his mouth, it was another count in the indictment. And in the planning of a crime, DePew was certainly in his métier. Between his zeal to be the expert, his antagonism to the class of fathers, his desire to verbalize violent fantasies in cinematic detail, and his hypercompensatory masculinity, there could not have been a more perfect marriage than this entrapment scheme and DePew's compulsive loquaciousness. His very *lack* of suspicion, his *lack* of paranoia, seems, in retrospect, pathological—an engraved invitation to bring punishment down upon himself.

DePew's boyish eagerness for technical know-how handed the prosecution what was likely the single most damaging piece of evidence against him. When various schemes to subdue the (still imaginary) child were discussed at the meetings, Dan, who claimed some familiarity with the techniques of anesthesia, volunteered to find out how to make chloroform. This interest in chloroform wasn't completely new for DePew. Part of his sexual repertoire included breath control—controlling someone's breathing or what they breathe. This included choking to the point of passing out, using implements like plastic bags, and occasionally using nitrous oxide—he had a tankful in his apartment, which he used during sex with Patrick, and which was seized after his arrest. (And which he didn't volunteer for the film, he points out.) "Why would anyone want to pass out during sex?" I asked, perhaps somewhat conventionally. Dan became positively rapturous explaining it to me. "Oh, you feel so great, it's like if your computer or TV is screwing up and you unplug it and plug it back in and then everything's fine—it's like all the worries and frustrations, and aggravations and screwed-up thoughts all get wiped clean. Like you've zapped the reset button and you wake up and you see all the most beautiful colors— more beautiful than you can describe. You wake up and you feel utterly wonderful and happy to be alive and really charged with life."

Breath control also means giving ultimate control to your top. "What do you feel emotionally about that person at that moment?" I asked him. "Oh, more than love," he says. "It's far more intense and far stronger than love. If you can keep your head in the right space, and he's good and can keep you there, it's like looking into heaven. It's nirvana, it's warmth, security, love, gratitude. . . . It's not sexual at all, I mean, that's part of it, because of the intensity of it all, but the only thing that exists is the immediate surroundings. You and your man."

According to DePew, following the conversation with the agents he became obsessed with the idea of trying out chloroform with Patrick. Thus, like the autodidact he is, and oblivious to the FBI agents trailing behind him everywhere he went,

Dan strolled to the library and looked it up. He also made calls to a couple of like-minded friends (recorded and subsequently introduced into evidence) to inquire if they knew anything about its chemical properties. For the government to prove conspiracy, there has to be at least one "overt act" in furtherance of the conspiracy. From their vantage point, the phone call and the trip to the library looked like the overt acts they needed.

A week after the four-way meeting, Bobby, now back in California, phones Ashley, who immediately informs him, "There's one small problem—I don't think they're gonna let me have vacation those two weeks." Bobby asks if Dave has looked into a vehicle and Dave says he hasn't had time. Bobby asks if he's bought muriatic acid, which was part of the plan. Ashley says he has, but when his house was searched after his arrest, none was found. It may be that Ashley was losing interest, or getting paranoid, or had never intended to go along with the plan at all. (DePew's lawyer, James Lowe—who would later go on to win the famous acquittal for Lorena Bobbitt—suggested in his closing that things were going beyond Ashley's fantasy and he wanted out.) Ashley would soon drop completely from sight. The difficulty of contacting him was a constant complaint of the other three, and it appears from the wiretap transcripts that during the nine days preceding his arrest Bobby couldn't reach him at all.

The two chat for about an hour, and Bobby dangles the prospect of various lucrative business schemes he says Roberto wants Dave to be part of. By the end of the conversation Dave is agreeing to try to get the time off work.

Next R.J. phones Dan DePew at work, soliciting his thoughts on their meeting. Dan offers that he wasn't too impressed with Ashley and R.J. quickly agrees that he hadn't been either—he calls Ashley the "master of double-talk." (For reasons that I never understood, the agents constantly trashed Ashley to DePew and vice versa. Perhaps it was because they understood that the two disliked each other and were trying to play along.) R.J. wants to know if Dan has looked into obtaining a vehicle and Dan says he hasn't. R.J. tells Dan that Ashley has been scouting around for one, which of course he hadn't. R.J. tells Dan he'll be back east in two weeks.

Bobby calls Ashley again. They mull over various business schemes, which Bobby tells Ashley boss Roberto will bankroll. Ashley seems enticed by the possibility of becoming a pornographic entrepreneur like Bobby, and like a couple of high rollers, they discuss the vast sums they'll soon be raking in. Ashley never seems to question why exactly these California pornographers need *him* in on these deals. Lamentably for DePew and Ashley, both seemed beset by fantasies of grandiosity, which the police manipulated like master puppeteers. It was *their* connections, *their* expertise that the two California pornographers couldn't proceed without. The loftiness of their fantasies prevented them from asking the most basic questions, from having the tiniest modicum of skepticism about how very improbable this whole setup was.

Another week passes. R.J. calls DePew again. DePew can't talk, but calls him back later that day and says, suddenly, "I've decided not to be involved." R.J., startled, responds, "You what?" Dan says again, "I've decided not to be involved in this one." R.J. seems at a loss for words. "You've decided not to be involved in this one?" he repeats. Dan goes on to complain about not having heard from Ashley, about not trusting Ashley, and about everything going too fast. DePew may have been attempting to disentangle himself, but legally speaking, it's not so easy to get out of a conspiracy. The only way to withdraw from a conspiracy, the judge would later tell the jury, is to actually do something to *defeat* the purpose of the conspiracy. The law demands heroism, and DePew, trying desperately not to piss anyone off, fell far short of the legalities of withdrawal—assuming that he was indeed legally a part of the conspiracy, which James Lowe later attempted to dispute. Instead of declaring his moral indignation and threatening to report the nefarious scheme to the police, he pussyfooted around and finally said that he was wary about not having known the two agents long enough, and suspicious of Ashley generally. Nervously attempting to appease R.J., he offered, "I'm still open-minded for one if we can develop a rapport, but this one I'm definitely passing on."

R.J. quickly shifts into damage-control mode, working every angle to lure DePew back into the fold. Would DePew go along with it if it were just the three of them? Maybe? Okay, here comes the guilt trip: "We were . . . we were really excited, I mean, we're planning, we've already got plans that we're coming out." He appeals to Dan to talk to Bobby, so Bobby can explain why Ashley hasn't called. Dan repeats his stand to Bobby: "I was just telling R.J. that I've decided not to be involved in this one. . . . I want to pass on this one." Bobby too works the angles. They've already made their plans to come, he says, and it's not just them but that "you know, part of the deal for us—the other people involved, you know," by which he seems to mean Roberto the mobster boss, which Dan took as a veiled threat. Bobby proposes, "Maybe we could still keep things going, but at a later date." R.J. gets back on the phone and reassures Dan that Ashley will call. He asks Dan to meet with them again when they come to D.C. Dan reluctantly agrees.

Having won one concession, R.J. pleads that Ashley has to stay in, for Bobby's sake. He tries a new approach: making Ashley the object of their shared aggression. "You know, I've always kinda kept my feelings pretty honest with you on how I felt about Dave," he tells Dan. "I figured that after we got done doing what we were gonna do with the kid, I'd take time to beat the shit outta Dave." This was a psychological master stroke, and with each complaint about Ashley, R.J. lulls Dan farther back in. After R.J. finishes denouncing Ashley, Dan concedes that he's still interested, but now deploys a new excuse: he can't possibly be ready in time. R.J. quickly agrees that it does need more planning. (The agents would obviously agree to anything, as long as they can keep some semblance of four-way involvement going.) R.J. suggests they go over the details more thoroughly on their next trip out. Dan protests that he doesn't want them to make a special trip just to talk, and he'd be willing to talk on the phone. R.J. insists that they're willing to do their part, which means flying back to the East Coast. Dan valiantly repeats that he doesn't want to be involved, and R.J. translates, "Well the current schedule is what you have a real problem with." Dan agrees. He offers that he'd be involved with the two of them, but not with Ashley. R.J. agrees and adds, "Personally, I wouldn't mind drop-kicking Dave through the goalposts of life," but now adopting a therapeutic approach, he advises that the best idea is for the four of them to sit down and work out their differences. He requests a favor from Dan: if Dan hears from Dave, R.J. asks him to call Bobby. In other words, keep in touch. Dan agrees.

Six days later R.J. calls Dan again. No, Dan still hasn't heard from Ashley. The agents hadn't heard from him either, although R.J. tells Dan that Bobby and Ashley have been playing phone tag on the answering machine. (In fact, they haven't been able to reach Ashley at all.) Dan turns the conversation to a detailed discussion of his company's takeover, then moves into an equally detailed discussion of Patrick's vacation to visit his family, then launches into a long disquisition on the possibility of controlling an ATM via his mainframe computer. (I noticed this too in talking with him: when he doesn't want to discuss something he talks at great length about something else.) R.J. wraps up the conversation by saying, "We just wanted to let you know we're dead serious. Pun intended." He tells Dan they're still planning on coming out the following week and asks if he can meet. Dan says he can get away for a couple of hours and tries to tell him when, but R.J. cuts him off with, "What we'd like to see is if you've got any ideas. Maybe this time we'd like to go check them out, some of the places." Dan says okay and adds something about "dry runs" being a good idea, but whether he was agreeing to participate or just trying to get off the phone is open to interpretation. (The state would later successfully argue that "dry run" meant kidnapping a child.)

Five days later the FBI showed up and arrested Dan at work. Dean Lambey was arrested the same day.

Henry Hudson, the U.S. attorney for eastern Virginia, called a press conference to announce the arrests. Hudson had, coincidentally, been chairman of the 1986 Attorney General's Commission on Pornography, which released a widely criticized 1,960-page report (the infamous "Meese Report") linking pornography to sexual violence. He'd become a controversial figure in his previous job as commonwealth's attorney in Arlington because members of the Arlington police department were in the curious habit of encouraging prostitutes to travel to Arlington, Virginia, from Washington and as far away as Baltimore and then arresting them for solicitation. Critics accused Hudson of importing crimes solely for the purposes of prosecuting them, charging that Hudson was using police resources to advance his own career. Hudson did have a reputation for ambitiousness. Within a year of becoming U.S. attorney, his office became the first in the country to use RICO statutes for obscenity cases, allowing the government for the first time to seize assets in pornography prosecutions. (He also had a reputation for playing hard-core pornography at office parties, attorney James Lowe told me, on the record.)

Reporters gathered for the press conference having been told by Hudson's office that Hudson would be making an announcement of national importance. Hudson, joined by the two FBI branch heads from the Washington and Richmond offices, announced the arrests of Lambey and DePew, but provided only the barest outline of the case. (He did announce that because Dean Lambey had discussed the possibility of using his own house for the filming, application had been made to have the house seized by federal marshals and made subject to forfeiture.) But he answered almost every other question with, "I can't discuss that."

Reporters began to balk. What was of national importance here—wasn't this a local crime? Of course everyone knew that the previous month a ten-year-old Fairfax County girl had been kidnapped and murdered, and this case couldn't help but be associated with that one. "Parents should exercise caution concerning their children's whereabouts," Hudson said. "There are, as this case illustrates, people out there who choose to prey on children." "Was this a widespread problem?" he was asked. Hudson assured them that it wasn't. "But if they aren't a widespread problem, and it's just one case that you have in northern Virginia, then why put parents on alert and have them worry about a situation that's not a major or widespread problem anyway?" a reporter pressed. Hudson refused to answer this or any other question put to him about the case. However, the press conference was dutifully reported, and as more lurid details were released the media gratefully lapped them up.

DePew's encounter with the criminal justice system was a series of fatal missteps and mutual noncomprehension. When taken to FBI headquarters, he, quite stupidly thinking it was Bobby and R.J. who were the targets, cooperated fully. He didn't initially ask for a lawyer; he says when he finally did, they told him they wouldn't be able to get him one that day. They explained to him what conspiracy was, told him that Bobby, R.J., and Ashley had all been arrested, and that whoever talked first got the deal. He spent four hours talking to them. When the two FBI agents doing the interrogation did the good cop/bad cop routine, he, of course, developed an instant crush on the bad cop and talked even more. DePew seems to have had a problem understanding that the FBI agents weren't on his side; his overidealization of masculine authority was once again his downfall.

In DePew's account of the interrogation he asked for a lawyer, and he didn't confess to intending to make a snuff film (although he said that he believed Bobby and R.J. were serious about it). However, in Special Agent Barry Kroboth's account of the interrogation, DePew confessed to having unquestionably intended to make a snuff film.

Kroboth testified in court that the interview wasn't taped. DePew says he thought it was being taped. Although at the pretrial hearing to quash the confession Kroboth said, "There was no tape recorder in the room," at the trial he stated, "There was a Superscope recorder [an audio recorder] sitting on the table." DePew too says there was a tape recorder in the middle of the table. Given that there was also a video camera in the room, it seems odd for the interview not to have been either audio- or videotaped—for what purpose were the machines in the interrogation room if not to tape interrogations and confessions? Of course, if DePew *had* asked for a lawyer and not been provided one (and had this request been taped), it would most likely have made any subsequent "confession" inadmissible.

In the defense pretrial motion to dismiss the confession, the judge ruled, not surprisingly, that FBI Agent Kroboth's testimony was more credible than gay sadomasochist DePew's. What this meant was that DePew's confession, as related by Kroboth, was admissible at the trial, and the only record of this confession was in Kroboth's written notes. These notes, riddled with inconsistencies, were Kroboth's "conclusions" rather than a verbatim record, and didn't even cover the entire interrogation. DePew, who struck me as remarkably without bitterness about his arrest and imprisonment, is vocally bitter about only one aspect of the case: Kroboth's testimony.

Lowe made a second pretrial motion disputing that there was ever a viable conspiracy. He argued that there was no agreement to anything at Lambey's preliminary meeting with DePew in the Alexandria hotel, and that at the first meeting between DePew and the two agents, DePew had explicitly told the agents he had no agreement with Lambey. (This *is* on tape.) Thus there couldn't have been a conspiracy prior to the second meeting between the four men. (Kroboth's notes claimed, however, that DePew confessed that he left the Alexandria meeting having agreed to make a snuff film with Lambey. This is one reason the admissibility of Kroboth's notes was such a calamity for the defense.) The judge interjected that a "tacit understanding" was enough to qualify as conspiracy. Lowe continued what was by now looking like a losing argument, claiming that at the second meeting there was discussion without any agreement to do anything. The judge ruled that the conspiracy began with DePew and Lambey's meeting at the Alexandria hotel. Things went swiftly downhill from there.

DePew's essential problem at the trial was translating what are, essentially, subcultural practices and interests to a group of outsiders who find them foreign and repellent. The prosecution had a fairly easy task. All they had to do was paint DePew as a brutal and monstrous figure and convince the jury that consensual sadomasochism constituted hard evidence that DePew intended, without a doubt, to commit kidnapping and child murder. They introduced items seized from DePew's home into evidence: nooses, hooks, ropes, manacles, leather straps, leather masks, paddles with metal studs, pictures of men in bondage, books about bondage, pictures of DePew's bedroom, and videotapes of consensual S&M between DePew and different lovers. After all, why would someone consent to be burned with a cigarette, or strangled, or beaten (all portrayed in stills of DePew in sexual activity shown to the jury) unless he was also going to kill a child? They stressed that since DePew's sadomasochistic sexual practices were "real," not fantasy, the snuff film plot was real as well. Regarding his sex life with Patrick, DePew was asked, "When you hang someone, you actually do that, don't you?" DePew answered yes. "It's not a fantasy?" DePew agreed that it was not. "When you strangle someone, you actually do that. It's not a fantasy, correct?"

DePew was able to win one small point about fantasy when a video was played for the jury in which the camera pans through a park, with DePew's voice-over saying, "This is where I come to find my boys and kill my boys." Prosecuting attorney Neil Hammerstrom demands, "Now, how can you tell this jury now that you have no interest in children?" DePew answers, "Because to me a boy does not have to be a child. A boy can be any age. Patrick, my lover, is my boy, and I refer to him as 'my boy.'" Hammerstrom: "Do people Patrick's age play in playgrounds?" DePew answers that they do, and points out that if they watched the rest of the tape, it portrayed *Patrick*—six foot three, with a mustache, and in his late twenties—swinging on a swing in the playground, not a child. DePew may have won the skirmish, but he was still hopelessly tainted with the stain of perversity. The state's larger point was that anyone weird enough to make that tape and do all the rest of the sordid things he'd done was weird enough to do anything, and this point seems to have prevailed. Hammerstrom even questioned DePew about having converted from Southern Baptist to Mormonism (which he had, believing it was more enlightened toward homosexuality) and demanded, "Do you believe that the Mormon religion recognizes sadomasochism?" Hammerstrom seemed to take offense at DePew's statement that he'd developed his own special relationship with God, and asked him twice if he actually believed that.

James Lowe says he had a pretty good idea that things weren't going well. Throughout the trial it seemed like the government lawyers had more success in creating a coherent narrative, in selling their version of the story. One reason was monetary: the government spent a fortune on this case. When I asked Officer James Rodrigues how much the investigation had cost, he put the out-of-pocket expenses alone at $300,000, not including man-hours, which would have more than doubled that amount. The two San Jose officers spent over six months on the case. At the height of the investigation there were over a hundred FBI agents assigned to the case, doing twenty-four-hour-a-day surveillance for almost a month. There were two assistant U.S. attorneys prosecuting the case, with an untold number of research staff and assistants behind them. (It shows in their briefs, which cite scores of precedents for every point and are most elegantly written, as opposed to Lowe's one-man productions.) Between the six-month setup on the West Coast, the massive FBI gala on the East Coast, and the trial, it's likely the government sunk at least $1 million into the case against Lambey and DePew. By contrast, Lowe was operating on a shoestring: his fee was $25,000—in terms of current legal costs, close to nothing. It's interesting to speculate on how this trial would have turned out had DePew had the government's limitless resources —or even O. J. Simpson's—for his defense.

Lowe's main point was that DePew knew where the line between fantasy and reality was, and was in it for the fantasy. It was the *agents*, he said, who failed to make the distinction between fantasy and conspiracy. This explanation never strongly took hold with the jury. Lowe emphasized throughout the trial that DePew was, yes, a sadomasochist, but he wasn't a pedophile.

There was no evidence that he had any interest in real children. This distinction also seems to have been lost. Lowe introduced testimony about the sadomasochistic subculture, about the practice of setting and adhering to rules and limits, about the importance of fantasy. He insisted that DePew had never inflicted any actual harm on anyone and that all his sex partners were still alive and kicking. The violent details DePew went on about were just "hot talk" designed to interest Bobby and R.J. sexually and get them into bed. Yes, fantasy involves a certain amount of reality, and yes, DePew was into bizarre stuff, and yes, he knows he represents the most unpopular defendant who will be tried in the state of Virginia that year, and he knows that DePew "is involved in almost every area that turns people off." But they can't decide the case on the basis of being horrified by DePew's sex life.

Or can they? U.S. Attorney Mike Smythers rebutted Lowe's closing argument by first avowing that DePew wasn't on trial for homosexuality or sadomasochism, but then following up with, "S&M in this trial doesn't mean sadomasochism. What it really means is Satan and Murder." He said he didn't want to put DePew on trial for S&M, but then said, of DePew's homemade sex videotapes that *weren't* introduced as evidence, "The other videotapes would have been enough to gag a maggot, to be quite honest about it, and we didn't want to prejudice you. . . ." (This was his somewhat feeble explanation of why the prosecutors didn't reveal to the jury that it was Patrick in the tape filmed in the park.) "S&M," he continued, "while they try to act like this is normal because maybe it's normal for them, it is still filled with violence and it's brutal and it's ugly." He repeated that he was not trying to play on the jury's prejudices, but then, referring to Lowe's argument that DePew was merely fantasizing, he demanded, "Who wants to put their child up first? Which child do we turn over to him to test this and see if he's actually going to carry this through? Do we want to take that kind of chance in our society? No!" Daniel DePew, he sputtered, "would have made a good first assistant for Josef Mengele or Adolf Eichmann."

The jury began deliberating at 2:15 in the afternoon. An hour later they sent a note out asking for the definition of conspiracy. They took a break from 4:45 to 5:00. At 6:15 they asked to see a videotape of DePew hanging Patrick, a request the judge denied because the prosecution, although they'd played it, hadn't entered it into evidence. Ten minutes later they announced they'd reached a verdict and returned to the courtroom. DePew stood, trembling, and faced the jury. As the guilty verdict was read, tears filled his eyes. A moment later he sat down and put his head in his hands.

After the jury was dismissed, the forewoman, Cathy Boehme, told reporters that DePew's homosexuality and sado-masochism had no bearing on their decision. "We separated out his sexual preference," she said. "The question was, Did he really fantasize the killing of a child or did he really mean it?" She added that during the three-day trial, DePew appeared "benign and didn't necessarily look like the stereotype who could plan such a horrible crime."

At the sentencing hearing, Judge T. S. Ellis, addressing DePew, pronounced his "the most heinous crime I have presided over." Then, oddly, he added, echoing forewoman Boehme, "The paradox is that you at one time present this embodiment of evil. . . . There is no doubt in my mind that you intended to commit the crime. The paradox is that as this chilling picture of evil is presented, there is also, strangely enough, almost a sympathetic . . . it's difficult to explain." Judge Ellis must have been responding to what I too encountered in DePew: a very basic and overwhelming gentleness. He conveys a certain slightly apologetic dignity about being who he is, as if he knows he got stuck with a bad deal but is trying hard to make the best of it.

Of course, DePew didn't make that impression on everyone. U.S. Attorney Hammerstrom actually tried to get the judge to increase the sentence to life strictly on the basis of DePew's sadomasochism, telling the judge (referring to the videos), "When Mr. Smythers told the jury that there was enough in there to gag a maggot, that was no overstatement. Many of us who had to watch these videos nearly lost our lunch. They were gruesome." Judge Ellis responded irritably, "Why in the world is that necessary to mention at this point? What's that got to do with sentencing?" Hammerstrom tried again: "Because, Your Honor, this man is so depraved that if he would engage in this kind of activity—" Ellis interrupted, "That isn't what he was tried and convicted for." Of course Ellis then turned around and meted out the thirty-three-year sentence, rejecting any argument for leniency or reduction in the sentencing level. Instead he added two levels because the *fictive* intended victim was a child.

There had been an extensive and complicated argument about the applicable sentencing level, with DePew ultimately sentenced on the basis of conspiracy to both kidnap and murder (he hadn't been charged with conspiracy to murder) because the government argued that murder was part of the kidnapping plot. On every question regarding sentencing, the judge found for the state. He also stated quite vehemently that he didn't believe DePew was looking for a way out, didn't believe that he was trying to withdraw from the conspiracy in the phone call in which he told R.J. and Bobby he wanted out, and that there was no doubt in his own mind that DePew and Lambey would have ultimately carried out the scheme. He also believed that DePew was completely without remorse. If he'd found that DePew accepted responsibility for the crime, it could have meant a two-level reduction, but DePew continued to insist that he never intended to carry out the crime, and the judge refused the reduction. Mandatory sentencing guidelines (without possibility of parole) have made federal prisons long-term warehouses. At Ray Brook, where DePew is now imprisoned, the average sentence is twelve years.

With a thirty-three-year sentence, DePew is watching men who have actually committed murder, rape, and child molestation getting out far sooner than he, who merely fantasized about it.

Dean Lambey, who seems to have gotten some spectacularly bad legal counsel, pleaded guilty rather than go to trial, following Richmond attorney William Linka's advice that he would get a seven-to-ten-year sentence. (Linka told me that Lambey had been promised leniency for cooperation.) Instead, U.S. district judge Richard L. Williams sentenced him to thirty years in jail. (James Lowe says contemptuously that Linka either misunderstood or didn't read the federal sentencing guidelines.) Lambey fired Linka and tried to withdraw his guilty plea. Not so fast, said the court. The case went immediately to a federal appeals court, where the plea and the sentence were upheld, although five of the thirteen judges dissented. U.S. Attorney Hammerstrom, zealously taking advantage of every opportunity to inflict the greatest degree of punishment possible, argued at DePew's sentencing hearing that "justice dictates" that DePew be given an even harsher sentence than Lambey.

Clearly the sadomasochistic fantasies circulating through the DePew case weren't DePew's alone: they permeated the entire case from beginning to end, just as they permeate the cultural imagination. What were the fantasies and ambitions of the two undercover cops playing the roles of tough-guy pornographers, inventing lurid sex scenes with which to regale Ashley and DePew? When DePew joined them in a hotel room to spin out tall tales of sex and violence in what he initially thought was going to be a seduction scene, weren't they all doing the same thing—lying to get their man? In magnifying those rambling stories of DePew's into evidence of intent, the prosecution deliberately overlooked just how common fantasy and hyperbole are when it comes to sex: certainly at this very moment people are lying and exaggerating in order to get someone into bed in hotel rooms around the world. Did the prosecution imagine that pillow talk is conducted under oath?

Sadomasochism, as practiced by Daniel DePew and his friends, is a distinct subculture, with its own rules and etiquette, its own customs, values, and language. As with any subculture, these rules are agreed on and adhered to by the members of the group. To the sadomasochistic cognoscenti, violent fantasies are foreplay, not conspiracy. For the state to peremptorily redefine minority subcultural practices according to its own say-so would seem like a form of cultural violence were it directed at a more popular or politically powerful group than gay sadomasochists. Even Santeria religious animal slaughter won Supreme Court protection against the city of Hialeah, which had attempted to outlaw it (despite the fact that the slaughter of animals by the beef and poultry industries thrives freely in mainstream culture). Subcultural practices often look weird from the outside, to noninitiates, but they receive certain forms of protection and recognition as cultural expression.

Sadomasochism, for DePew, *was* a form of cultural expression. Culture isn't only mass-produced, the product of multinational entertainment conglomerates, and we're not only passive recipients. We make our own culture as well. DePew had literary aspirations as a writer of fantasy: he frequently took requests to custom-write erotic stories for others on computer bulletin boards. He's written a 270–page novel with similar themes. But of course DePew didn't single-handedly invent the genre of the violent fantasy: our cultural products in general are increasingly soaked in blood. Had DePew had the cultural capital, or even the arrogance, to declare himself an artist maybe he could have been a Wes Craven or even an Oliver Stone instead of a midlevel electronics worker with an unorthodox private life.

Culture—including pornography—is a place where problematic social issues get expressed and negotiated. In much the same way, DePew's private erotic theater also enacted a particular kind of problem-solving. It was, in a sense, scripted, with a repeating cast of characters in assigned roles and certain themes that were returned to again and again. These memorialized the injuries to masculinity and identity that had marked his early life, but also, with a brand of heroic optimism, attempted to cure them. The jury may have been disturbed by the theatrical violence of his sex life, but that violence had a complex history; it had a narrative.

These kinds of narratives animate the entire pornographic enterprise. As with other forms of culture—as with art or literature—we may be called upon to interpret, to read between the lines (or between the bodies), to perform acts of critical exegesis. As with other forms of culture to which we readily apply our interpretive capabilities, meanings don't necessarily sit on the surface announcing "Here I am." You may have to dig for them. They may take an allegorical form: as in the DePew case, a second level of meaning resides beneath what's explicit. In the genres of pornography discussed in the following chapters, the allegories are large-scale and culturally specific: pornography becomes a way to simultaneously ventilate and submerge problematic contents prohibited from expression in other public forums.

Pornography requires our interpretation, and in return it yields surprising eloquence. Eloquence needs to be pursued, even if it leads us to unlikely places. The criminal justice system disposed of Daniel DePew as quickly as it did because it refused the burdens of interpretation, it was only too willing to treat DePew as though he were some sort of single-celled organism. Plumbing any more deeply might have been disturbing, inconvenient.

The desperate quality to DePew's particular quest, along with its very ordinariness, strikes too close to the bone of ex-

actly those buried motifs most of us expend much of our psychic energies circumnavigating. As Freud points out, at the
bottom of all this theatricality is the banality of everyday unhappiness. Such are the longings, and injuries, and the small hu-
miliations that constitute us and that are perched forevermore
just at the edges of awareness, or redeemed within the private
utopias of our fantasies. As a culture, our intellectually shriveled
approach to pornography has similarly avoided any such disturbing acts of self-recognition: daring nothing, denying everything.
Daniel DePew's fantasies were at some level familiar, and all
too human: he became a sacrifice to our own defensive (and
overly optimistic) fantasies that we're not all cut from this very
same cloth.

Two

Clothes Make
the Man

Defining pornography is one big headache. One person's pornography is another person's erotica, and one person's erotica can cause someone else to lose her lunch. The celebrated dictum "I know it when I see it" made Supreme Court Justice Potter Stewart the subject of unremitting smirks and winks, and his flat-out admission of the complete subjectivity of the definitional enterprise only underlines its futility. But if for Daniel DePew pornographic fantasy had all the elements of cultural expression, what then *are* the distinctions between pornographic culture and the rest of what we call culture? Or rather, what impedes us from considering pornography as a mode of expressive culture? What disastrous thing would happen if we were to—just experimentally, provisionally—approach pornography as we would any other cultural form, applying to it the same modes of respectful analysis, the kind of critical attention received not infrequently by even the dumbest forms of mass culture? (Even *boxing* gets serious intellectual consideration.)

One impediment to such an experiment is the ascendancy of antipornography feminists, who have announced with great certainty what pornography is, with no room for such questions as these I'm posing. For these critics, pornography is defined by a particular form of gender relations, namely its mission to control and oppress women. Feminist Susan Gubar defines pornography as "a gender-specific genre produced primarily for men but focused obsessively on the female figure" and distinguished by its dehumanizing effect.[1] Catharine MacKinnon and Andrea Dworkin have famously defined pornography as the "graphic and sexually explicit subordination of women." And that lilting phrase "objectification of women" gets a lot of play in these discussions.

All of this is fairly familiar, but of course none of it is applicable to the pornography of *male* bodies, which is, by any definition, a substantial share of what gets bought and sold as pornography these days. Why has there been such reticence about dealing with the issues raised by pornography in which the bodies depicted are bodies possessing penises? Perhaps it's because doing so throws any certainty about what pornography is and does into question. Which is exactly why I bring it up, given that my intentions are to disrupt some of these assumptions about what pornography is and does. If you even tentatively acknowledge the possibility that "pornography" is a far from coherent or stable category, if you even fleetingly concede that its motives and purposes could be less black and white than "graphic subordination" or the "dehumanization of women," it becomes far more difficult to either employ it as a political rallying point or to hold it responsible for the range of social ills it now stands charged with causing.

Take transvestite pornography. While gender is definitely a central preoccupation of this genre, the particulars don't follow any of the standard presumptions about how pornography works and at whose expense. Transvestite porn, if it accomplishes anything, accomplishes the frustration of all wishes for stability and coherence. That is to say, it defies categories: the category of pornography, first off—if pornography is defined as having the ambition to oppress women. But more to the point, it even defies the conventional categories for making such easy gender classifications. The bodies portrayed here run the gamut from males to males dressed as females, to males with breasts and penises, along with a smattering of bossy-looking (biological) women. Some of the men are transvestites, some are transsexuals, some prefer women as sex partners, some like men, and some like either—depending on how you, or he, or both are dressed at the time.

For the sake of brevity I'm referring to this genre as "transvestite porn," but let me clarify: the term "transvestite" refers to men (I won't be discussing female transvestism here, although it does exist[2]) who dress in women's clothing, while the term "transsexual" refers to men who have physically changed their primary or secondary sexual characteristics through hormones or surgery—typically, in these magazines, men who have sprouted breasts through hormones or implants, but still have penises; that is, "preoperative" transsexuals. (This term too is somewhat misleading, because not all men with breasts and penises are actually headed for "the slice," or gender reassignment surgery, so they're not really "pre" anything.) The psychological literature insists that the difference between transvestites and transsexuals is that transvestites see themselves as men and want to be men, albeit men dressed occasionally as women, while transsexuals actually want to be women. But what these magazines indicate is that even this distinction is far from clear or even very distinct, and that there's quite a lot of blur to these desires and their modes of expression.

Sometimes the photographs in transvestite magazines are sexually explicit, but sometimes they're not explicit at all. A substantial number of the bodies portrayed are actually fully clothed—you'd have to look fairly closely to distinguish some of these photos from a harmless family snapshot of your Aunt Marge. (Or maybe Uncle Morris.) This raises yet another interesting category issue: Why does a fully dressed man— albeit one fully dressed as a woman—fall under the heading of "pornography"?

Yet despite these definitional conundrums, this kind of material is unproblematically classed as pornographic, and is often considered even *more* pornographic than run-of-mill "fuck and suck" pornography, at least in my area of the country. In Chicago, there's a tacit understanding on the part of most local porn businesses that carrying transvestite porn will get them raided by the local vice squad, working under the direction of the state's attorney's office. You can freely obtain magazines showing naked men, naked women, and any combination of them doing very acrobatic, unexpected, or sadomasochistic things to each other, but if one of the men is wearing a garter belt, apparently purveyors are subject to arrest and prosecution. Locals who wanted to buy magazines like *Gender Gap, Transvestites on Parade, Feminine Illusion, Guys in Gowns, Petticoat Impostors, Great Pretenders, Femme Mimics,* or *Humiliated Transvestites* can drive to Kenosha, just an hour away across the Wisconsin border, where apparently an entirely different set of community standards prevails.[3]

If a man in a dress is an obscenity, what exactly is at stake for the culture in legislating male fashion? Why this zeal to keep men in pants, and what investment do we have in producing— and patrolling—this border? And how is this border experienced by those who dwell in the shadow of the guardtower?

Transvestite magazines follow a fairly standard format, but let me describe a typical one for my nontransvestite reader. Each issue generally features one or two short stories, typically in which an unwilling man is forced through a variety of circumstances to dress in women's clothes. Sometimes this sartorial strong-arm will be another man, sometimes a woman—often a mother or older female authority figure. The clothes are described in elaborate and abundant detail—reading these stories is a fashion education if you've never paid much attention to the fine points of seamstress-craft, or don't know your tulle from your taffeta. Often these dress-up sessions lead to sex in various configurations with either another man or a dominant woman. There are also advice columns in which similar narratives are presented in the guise of letters.

Then there are, of course, pictorials of cross-dressed men and preoperative transsexual models, often in lingerie or various stages of deshabille. Some display their genitals, some hide them between their legs. Others are fully clothed. Sometimes the models are engaged in sex, alone or with others, sometimes the partners are other men, other transvestites, or sometimes women of the take-charge type. Some of these photos are in a sadomasochistic vein—leather corsets make frequent appearances—or other types of fantasy scenarios are enacted, like the French maid or the sexual novice. There are also scattered ads by professional female dominatrixes who grudgingly admit to being willing to consider applications from submissive men who need training and discipline.

While psychological literature typically insists that TVs (transvestites) are heterosexuals (transvestism is distinguished by fetishism of the female clothing, as opposed to gay drag, which is just dressing up as a woman to be more fabulous), bisexuality is the sexual norm in these magazines: a picture's captions or the short stories might insist that a man is heterosexual, but nevertheless, he often finds himself enticed into sexual hijinks by a beautiful transvestite or transsexual. The actual biological sex of your sex partner seems of less importance here than in most other social and sexual venues. While it's not really my purpose to attempt to distinguish between heterosexual and homosexual transvestism (why bother?), I do want to point out in passing that these magazines contradict most of the category distinctions maintained in clinical literature on transvestism— for example, the insistence on defining transvestism as exclusively heterosexual. Clinicians Robert Stoller and Louise Kaplan, both noted experts on "perversions," define male transvestism as a man fetishizing female clothing as a path to arousal but in which his sexual object choice is a woman; both Stoller and Kaplan define homosexual drag as nonfetishistic cross-dressing.[4]

But what these transvestite magazines indicate is that many men who cross-dress and define themselves as heterosexual *are* interested in sex with other men or cross-dressed men when they themselves are cross-dressed, although they may regard themselves and even their bodies and genitalia as female in those encounters. Fantasy is clearly a powerful thing if it allows you to reassign your own sex and bed different sexes than usual with merely a change of outfit. This version of sexuality, at least as far as the biological sex of one's object-choice goes, seems much more multivalent than the experts suggest. There is also in these magazines, clearly, homosexual fetishism of female clothing. But of course it's important to remember that pornography is a fantasy form, and if a gay man has fetishistic fantasies about women's clothes, or a straight man has fantasies about sex with beautiful transsexuals, it doesn't follow that we know what that means about anyone's actual sexual practices. As is indicated in the video *She-Male Voyager*, a witty drag remake of the classic Bette Davis tearjerker (which as a tale of transformation and loss makes an exemplary frame narrative), which contains *both* gay sex and heterosexual sex in the same video, adding to our category difficulties. Murmurs Charlotte, still garbed in a beaded black cocktail dress, garters, and a snood after a steamy episode of (safe) anal sex in which *she* penetrates *him*: "Jerry darling, I'm sure I saw the moon and the stars." His rueful reply: "I'm sure you did. I'm sure everyone's seen them now."

In addition to the pictorials in transvestite magazines there are numerous advertisements: for sexual services, videos, and other pornography; for hormone supplements, makeup and dress advice (videos like *The Art of Femininity,* which explores "all the ways that you can be a more beautiful and convincing transvestite" or *Take It Off: TV Hair Removal Guide*); for an array of expensive and probably useless products like breast enhancement creams or vitamin tablets formulated from various glands that claim to soften skin (Feminique, Mammary Plus, or Femglan, whose ingredients consist of "such things as raw ovary, raw gland concentrate, raw pancreas, kidney, pituitary, plus herbs"); and for a myriad of supplements, depilatories, and prosthetics ("Now you can look like a perfect lady wearing nothing more than panties and these beautiful . . . REALISTIC BREASTS!").

As in your average woman's magazine, there's a booming market in female appearance anxiety—whatever the biological sex of the individual experiencing it—and wherever it can be aroused, there's soon a product to capitalize on it. It's apparent from advice columns—many of which consist of the kind of remedial clothes, makeup, and behavioral advice you might encounter in *Sassy* or *Seventeen*—and from the stories, that many of these readers experience overwhelming anxiety over not being (or worrying that they're not) successful as women, which means seamlessly feminine. As in the woman's magazine, femininity is something to be strived for, worked at, and achieved after great travail. Any creeping traces of masculinity (unwanted hair, rough skin, figure problems) must be immediately countered with expensive, often painful measures (electrolysis, corseting, etc.).

To be female means to be in malaise, forever fretting that the world at large is handing down caustic judgments about your clothes or your figure; the combined sense of being on display and being found wanting seems to constitute the everyday trauma of womanhood. Even worse is the possibility of not being found sexually desirable by all. It's a fascinating bit of cultural datum that regardless of biological sex, femininity and insecurity are so joined at the hip.

In response, the TV community seems to have assimilated and reinvented variations on the numerous anxiety-alleviating forms of contemporary women's culture. All of those therapeutic countermeasures that trickled down to the culture at large from the consciousness-raising movement of seventies feminism reappear here in nonpoliticized and commercialized forms. Whereas consciousness-raising devoted itself to exploring the social roots of female appearance anxieties, now we have its second incarnation as for-sale therapeutics: self-help and self-acceptance literature, advice columns, and 900 numbers (pay-by-the-minute phone services) for makeup and clothes advice, networking, introductions, and psychological support.

Finally, the magazines contain a large number of photographic personal ads, which actually take up the majority of the pages. In fact, some of the magazines have no editorial content at all, but consist solely of advertisements and photo classifieds. It's this last aspect of these magazines, the photo classifieds, that raises some quite interesting definitional questions—questions that pertain to how we define the entire pornographic enterprise.

These personal ads are basically amateur self-portraits. Many seem to be taken with time lapse devices or remote shutter cables (which can sometimes be seen in the photos), although it's usually not possible to say when there's another person actually taking the photo. Most are reproduced in grainy black and white, although some are color. They're usually of a single figure, a man, in various types of dress or stages of undress, almost always sporting articles of female clothing or lingerie. Most of the men face the camera frontally, gazing into the lens, although expressions and poses vary considerably. The majority are full figure. Sometimes genitals are showing, sometimes an erection is prominent, sometimes the man makes a point of concealing his genitals between his legs and feminizing himself. In many cases the man is completely dressed as a woman and strikes a pose suggestive of various familiar female stereotypes— the movie starlet, the slut, the matron, the shy virgin, the maid, the good ole girl.

The ostensible purpose of these photos is to meet other people, often for sexual encounters. (They all list box numbers and the state the poser hails from, along with a brief caption— "TV Novice," "TV Seeks Understanding," "Affectionate Loving TV," "Passable and Quite Cute"—and a short description.) But at times they simply request friendship, advice, or correspondence. Often what the poser claims to be advertising for seems unlikely to meet with that response. For example, some ads consist simply of a torso, a body part, or the poser from behind, and in some the language of the ad is so vague—"Write and tell me about yourself!"—that it's far from clear who, and of what sex, or for what purpose, is meant to respond. Some of the photos seem deliberately comic, or even carnivalesque, with garish makeup jobs and precariously top-heavy outsize prosthetic breasts.

To what degree are these ads forms of self-display rather than solicitations for dates? Or to put the question another way, to what extent are these *aesthetic* rather than purposive acts? Perhaps I can bring the aesthetic issues farther into the foreground by pointing out the similarity of the transvestite classifieds to other forms of aesthetic and imaginative self-display, such as those found in the world of art, although comparing the transvestite classifieds to materials that look similar but circulate in other contexts, like the art world, raises, once again, nagging definitional questions about pornography. Perhaps it even, if only momentarily, shakes these photos out of any easy categorical certainty.

What happens if you consider the transvestite classifieds within the category of the self-portrait, a subgenre of Western art and aesthetics with antecedents in painting as far back as the fifteenth century, and which, as critic and art historian Barbara Rose puts it, records

> the artist's subjective feelings about himself—his conception of how he is perceived by his world and how he experiences himself within a specific social, political, economic, moral and psychological context. Self-portraits often include revealing subconscious clues to the artist's emotional state and inner drama.[5]

What differentiates transvestite self-portraiture from the art historical understanding of self-portraiture as an aesthetic act of self-definition? That is, what differentiates it other than our expectations about the meanings of these respective contexts, and our preconceptions about what we'll find there: in pornography one thing, in art another. Except that, of course, twentieth-century art has set itself the task of flamboyantly defying those preconceptions at each and every turn: ever since the invention of an avant-garde tradition, having our presumptions defied is one of the things we now expect serious art to accomplish.

But, you argue, this is mass-produced smut, not *art*. (Of course you'd be on thin ground if you argued that it's merely commerce, since it's not as if there's not an art *market*.) In response, let me point out that one of the fundamental aesthetic preconceptions long since overhauled during the century-long reign of the avant-garde is the whole notion of authorship, and with it, any expectation the art viewer might once have had for the presence of the "hand" of the artist in the work. Also in decline is the value once accorded to skill or craft, whether technical or aesthetic. A brief review of the highlights of twentieth-century art: from the incorporation of newspapers within painting by cubists (highly controversial in its day), or Duchamp's display of everyday items like urinals within the gallery space (even more controversial), to the gleeful appropriation of anonymous mass cultural icons by pop artists, to the blank prefab constructions of the minimalists, to the "factory produced" paintings of Andy Warhol, up to and including the assembly-line techniques of current art world luminaries like Mark Kostabi or Jeff Koons—what now constitutes "art" is anyone's guess, but it doesn't depend on uniqueness, originality, or "aura."[6] Perhaps it *is* only a question of preconceptions. Or context.

If this is the case—if it's primarily issues of context and their concomitant preconceptions that create the "art experience"—what if we *were* to approach materials like the transvestite self-portraits with the same kinds of expectations that we bring to the museum or gallery: the anticipation of aesthetic shocks and visual pleasures, of a descent into symbolic language, of access to another consciousness, of a revealing exposure of our own lives and culture? Would we then find in them something similar to the kind of experience we glean from "art"?

Maybe it would help answer this question if we take a brief detour through the work of a well-known contemporary artist who has herself made a career of photographic self-portraiture: Cindy Sherman. Sherman became one of the best-known artists of her generation beginning in the early eighties, and following a series of photographs she produced called *Untitled Film*

Stills. In them she transforms herself into a variety of female types—The Girl Detective, America's Sweetheart, The Young Housewife, The Starlet, The Whore with a Heart of Gold, The Girl Friday, The Girl Next Door—by archly posing herself within the *mise-en-scènes* of nonexistent B-movies. To call these photographs "self-portraits" raises a definitional dilemma for the traditional conception of the self-portrait: although they are all "of" Sherman, the question is, who exactly is this "self"? As critic Arthur Danto puts it in the introduction to a coffee-table-size book of her photographs, "They are portraits at best of an identity she shares with every woman who conceives the narrative of her life in the idiom of the cheap movie."[7]

At first glance, the similarities between Sherman's work and the TV self-portraits are striking: both put categories of identity into question by using the genre of the self-portrait to document an invented "self." And both crucially concern themselves with the question of femininity and its masquerades. Arthur Danto's critical essay on Cindy Sherman's work makes a convenient jumping-off point to explore this rapport between pornography and art, all the more so because Danto, an aesthetician and critic, is concerned (as are we) with the question of how we arrive at categories and classifications in the arts.

Although he doesn't bother with the question "Is it art?" Danto instead demands of Sherman's photos "Is it photography?" given that Sherman isn't particularly concerned with the standard concerns of the art photograph such as print quality. Further, the genre she's chosen to appropriate—the film still—is what Danto labels "working photographs." He includes under this rubric the kinds of photographs that have a *purpose*, and are meant to perform some labor—photos that are "subartistic." Danto finally does concede, on two different grounds, that Cindy

Bound and Gagged

Sherman *is* a photographer. First, because the camera is central to her work, and the work draws on the language of photography. But more interestingly, Danto admits that the prejudice against "working photographs" is the basis of a class system in photography, in which an "aristocracy of proto-paintings" is allowed to lord it over "a proletariat of working photographs" that are actually often more meaningful to our everyday lives. For Danto, it was the political and aesthetic upheavals of the sixties that allowed these working photos to be perceived as vehicles for conveying meaning, and allowed everyday, unambitious photographs—baby pictures, graduation photos—to be taken seriously within an art context. These ordinary photos carry a "powerful charge of human meaning" because they "condense the biographies of each of us." It's now possible to "recognize the deep human essence with which these lowly images were steeped, aesthetics be damned."

What Danto makes clear is that refusing to take non-aristocratic, non–high art photographs seriously, or refusing to work as hard at extrapolating the kinds of meanings and affective impact from "lowly images"—say, transvestite self-portraiture—as from, say, Cindy Sherman's work, means imposing a pernicious and outdated class system on the field of photography. But it also means that you miss out on the "powerful charge of human meaning" that these lowly images convey. You miss learning the important things they have to say about our lives and our culture. So for Danto, once having established to his own satisfaction that Sherman can indeed be considered a photographer, Sherman's work becomes rich with meaning, not so much in terms of its aesthetic qualities, but in its themes, and its relation to its own culture and its audience. Sherman achieves

a oneness with her culture, a oneness with a set of narrative structures instantly legible to everyone who lives in this culture, and so a oneness with her presumed audience. The stills acquire consequently a stature as art which draws together and transcends their artistic antecedents. . . . [They] condense an entire drama. (13)

Given the aesthetic green light from Citizen Danto to look more deeply at the meanings residing within nonaristocratic photography, let's begin by asking, Just how different *are* Cindy Sherman's self-portraits from transvestite self-portraiture? How different are the kinds of relations Sherman's photos establish with their audience—the way that they're "instantly legible to everyone who lives in this culture," or the way they "condense an entire drama"—from the audience-photograph relationship established by transvestite self-portraiture? Don't the TV photos also, quite resonantly, evoke in any viewer a deeply internalized cultural memory bank of images and codes having to do with femininity? And aren't these photos only "legible" to the extent that the viewer recognizes and shares the gender and dress codes in operation? To just about any member of Western culture these photos are not only instantly recognizable, but probably quite aesthetically jarring. They're a blatant act of transgression against something most of us feel quite deeply (although may not be able to articulate on the spot)—the expectation of a natural equivalence between sex and gender. Meaning, if you have a penis, you're supposed to dress and act like a man. Isn't that the way it's supposed to be?

Well, maybe not, these photos are at pains to inform us. We're all quite well acquainted with the set of arbitrary signifiers—dress, hair, makeup, body language—that, when everything's working as it "should," make sex and gender *seem* equivalent, seem "natural." We in the nontransgendered population generally don't devote much thought to why we assume you can tell a person's sex by looking at his or her clothes, or why there's something that seems not quite right about a man in a beaded evening gown. Until we're forced to, say by the aesthetic shocks that transvestite self-portraits administer. Even more so than in Sherman's work—which is often critically celebrated for containing just this sort of insight—the viewer of transvestite self-portraiture is ushered toward a heightened critical awareness of the cultural construction of the feminine, precisely because in these transvestite photos, the bearer of the "codes" of femininity is—and often explicitly displays the fact that he is—biologically male.

Clearly this work too, as Sherman's is said to do, "condenses an entire drama," and a universal drama at that: the drama of gender assignment. What we see here, and see revealed in our own discomfort with these images—in our nervous joke, or in our easy contempt (the "we" here is the nontransgendered viewer)—is that the "ordinary" sometimes takes a tragic turn. As these brief glimpses into the occasional yet recurring cleavage between biological sex and binary gender reveal so well. One of the demands of great art, according to Danto, is that it "embody transformative metaphors for the meaning of human reality," and he sees Sherman's work as embodying such metaphors. But certainly these transvestite self-portraits embody nothing if not transformative metaphors; they too "require great courage," and they too "set up perturbations across a social field," which are a few of the other proofs of artistic greatness Danto applies to Sherman's photography. "The Girl," he writes, "is an allegory for something deeper and darker in the mythic unconscious of everyone, regardless of sex." Can't the same be said of the Petticoat Impostor?

Where Danto seems to miss the critical boat is in his insistence that the greatness of Sherman's work is the way that it addresses us in "our common humanity," the way it says "something profound about the feminine condition" yet touches us at a level "beyond sexual difference." What level is that? When are we beyond sexual difference? Here's a clue: psychoanalyst Louise Kaplan points out that the transvestite also desires a position beyond sexual difference. Kaplan's general view of perversions is that they're not simply sexual pathologies; rather, they're pathologies of gender role identity. What they represent is an inability to completely conform to the gender conventions and gender stereotypes of the dominant social order. Perversions are mental strategies that use

> one or another social stereotype of masculinity and femininity in a way that deceives the onlooker about the unconscious meanings of the behaviors she or he is observing. Were we to think about perversion solely in terms of manifest behaviors without going into the motives that give meaning to those behaviors, we could simply conclude that the male perversions are quests for forbidden sexual pleasures and nothing more.[8]

These transvestite personals then, would be narratives of gendering, rather than sexual come-ons. All "perverse scenarios," for Kaplan, are ways of triumphing over childhood traumas; male perversions allow men to cope with forbidden and humiliating feminine strivings and longings. Perversions are also a series of deceptions: the perverse strategy is to give vent to one forbidden impulse as a way of masking an even more shameful or dangerous one. This is a betting man's strategy, a wager that the desire that's out in the open will deflect the observer from the thing that's hidden. A male transvestite, in Kaplan's view, doesn't want to *be* a women, but is coping with forbidden feminine longings and the insurmountable anxiety they cause, by demonstrating that he *can* be a woman, but a woman with a phallus. A woman who hasn't been castrated. Cross-dressing is a performance of a script that allows a man to allay the anxiety of his feminine wishes, and this is particularly the case when, for whatever reason, there's been an incomplete adaptation to the social gender binary of masculinity.

Kaplan believes that transvestites are attracted to elaborate, theatrical forms of feminine display as a way of denying sexual difference. Perhaps this is not entirely unlike the attraction of a male viewer to the Cindy Sherman oeuvre, concerned as her work is, also, with elaborate and theatrical forms of feminine display. Here's a clue as to why a critic might insist, against all evidence, that these photos are *not* about sexual difference: the denial of sexual difference is part of the perverse scenario. No aspersion meant on Danto: one of the things I'm about to suggest is that art, and even art criticism, is never entirely nonperverse. Or to borrow Kaplan's language, it's comprised of perverse *strategies*.

According to Kaplan, female perversions reside in behaviors that exaggerate femininity; that is, in behaviors often seen as "normal" female conduct. (This is one reason perversion has been generally thought to be a male domain—we were overlooking their specifically female incarnations.) So were Cindy Sherman's adoption of stereotypically feminine behaviors, poses, and clothing presented outside the context of the art gallery; the clinical term "homovestism" might apply, which refers to a gender impersonation of a same-sex person, a way of acting out gender conflicts through dressing in exaggerated or ritualized versions of same-sex clothing.[9] Sherman, if you ran into her in a dark alley, might seem—given her repetitive return to the same "script" and without the license afforded by the designation "artist"—as perverse in her preoccupations as any cross-dresser.

According to Robert Stoller, the "scripts" behind perverse scenarios are similar to all instances of sexual excitation. Behind every erection, male or female, are fantasies—

meanings, scripts, interpretations, tales, myths, memories, beliefs, melodramas, and built like a playwright's plot, with exquisite care, no matter how casual and spontaneous the product appears. In this story—which may take form in a daydream as one's habitual method of operation for erotic encounters, in styles of dress and other adornments, in erotic object choice, and in preference in pornography (in brief, in any and all manifestations of erotic desire)—I shall keep insisting that *every detail counts*.[10]

For Stoller, sexual excitation, whether perverse or quotidian, has an aesthetics that is as complex, coded, and loaded with meaning as other forms of narrative, theater, or art. Perverse scenarios are particularly tightly constructed: every detail and element is fraught with narrative significance. It's like an art form. Indeed, the language Stoller uses to describe the aesthetics of perversions, to trace their origins and describe their biographical raw materials, is almost identical to the type of language used by psychologically minded art critics to describe the aesthetic and creative process of the modern artist.

Artistic creativity, and the specific repetitions within an individual artist's oeuvre that constitute style, thematics, even medium, are often said to have their formation in unconscious, unresolved conflicts, traumas, and torments that get expressed, returned to, and repeated in art and literature. It may be something of a critical cliché in the age of the death of the author, but the artist as suffering neurotic is still one of the most prevalent explanations of the mysteries of artistic production. (Isn't this the basis of the huge biography industry on writers and artists?) Here, for example, is one art historian's analysis of painter Piet Mondrian's abstractions:

> Mondrian's aesthetic choices emerged from his unconscious conflicts; as he translated these choices into his

painting, wielding his ruler and applying his brush, these conflicts guided his hand. He found sensuality so frightening that it was his dread of desire, rather than the desires themselves, that ultimately shaped his abstract designs. No sentiment, no curves, no touching—that is how he lived and that is what his paintings proclaim. . . . [They] offer impressive evidence of just how much beauty the talented can wrest from fear. . . . Painting was, for Mondrian, the aesthetic correlative for his repressions, his way of coming to terms with himself—at once an expression of his problem and an embodiment of his solution.[11]

And who among us hasn't made the same sort of casual inference about an artist, writer, or filmmaker's unconscious life and preoccupations, as read through the symptoms displayed in his or her work? Just think of Alfred Hitchcock, and the booming cottage industry devoted to linking his psychosexual quirks to the thematics of his films. Sublimation, which in its pop-psychology form means "working something out" through other means, is regularly acknowledged by both professional and casual critics as the key to artistic production: socially unacceptable impulses and contents are channeled through and buried in the artistic work for future critics and historians to interpret.

As perversion starts to appear more aesthetic—"every detail counts" as Robert Stoller tells us—do aesthetics, conversely, start to seem just a tiny bit more perverse?

In Freudian theory proper, the *what* that gets channeled elsewhere, into these more socially valued forms, is libido. Freud himself explicitly connected art and perversion: "The forces that can be employed for cultural activities are thus to a great extent obtained through the suppression of what are known as the *perverse* elements of sexual excitation." These are what Freud referred to as the component instincts, which are anarchic, polymorphous, and infantile, and which, when they fail to achieve successful integration into normal adult sexuality, are most likely to become sublimated into other aims.[12] (And don't forget the connection between "sublimation" and the sublime.) So art and perversion are similar in origin, dissimilar in that art rechannels the same impulses and energies into a more socially acceptable or elevated idiom: aesthetic language.

This rechanneling means that, on the surface, art tends to *look* different than perversion, or its commodity form, hard-core pornography. Stoller defines pornography as material that intends to be pornographic; that is, that intends to produce a certain response—arousal—in its audience. But at the same time, for Stoller, art and pornography are quite formally similar: he repeatedly points out that erotic response is as complex a phenomenon as aesthetic response. The distinctions between the two come down to differences in their respective contents.[13] But as we've seen, there are many similarities: not only can an art photograph look a lot like a photograph that appears in a porn magazine, but art is libidinal and perverse, while perversions have their own aesthetic codes. And both are structured according to the imperatives of the unconscious. Perversion, having undergone mutation in the psychic process of sublimation, in turn becomes the basis for what we know as "aesthetic response."[14]

Perhaps we're devoted to keeping art and pornography so discursively sequestered exactly because aesthetics and perversity are so contiguous (and perhaps, contagious)—which is why it might seem like an important thing to firmly differentiate a Cindy Sherman photograph in which there's a gender impersonation of a movie starlet from a transvestite self-portrait in which there's a gender impersonation of a movie starlet. If the aesthetic response is actually completely *dependent* on perversity, and aesthetics has its origin in the alchemy between sublimation and perversion—as Freud suggests—then this somewhat demotes the status of the aesthetic. It starts to seem a bit of a lower thing, maybe not any better than a bottom-of-the-heap thing like pornography. This would be bad, because aesthetics is nothing if not status conscious. And, of course, the connection between aesthetics and class is something that hardly needs going into: aesthetics permeates every aspect of the entire social-class-distinction-making enterprise.

The class issues involved in the aesthetics-sublimation process aren't something that get much play in either psychoanalytic approaches to perversion or in the literature of aesthetics. Sublimation takes a certain amount of cultural competence. The skills necessary to do the work of translating the energies of compulsion and perversion into the lofty heights of aestheticism and the language of form are largely dependent on education and ease in the world of cultural endeavors. It presupposes a degree of intellectualization and the "distance from the world" that, as French sociologist Pierre Bourdieu writes, is the basis of the bourgeois experience.[15] There may be upper-class aesthetes using porn or lower-class abstract artists producing high-priced gallery art, but generally, according to Bourdieu, artistic competence and the "aesthetic disposition" get produced via what he refers to as "educational capital"—itself a mechanism for enforcing class distinctions.

So, inherent in these categorical distinctions between art and pornography are the class divisions that a distinctively high art works to maintain. Then there's the fact that sublimating real-world concerns into aesthetics, and particularly into abstraction, tends to invite contemplation of the results, as opposed to any sort of action—distance as opposed to engagement. As art historian Francis O'Connor writes of Mondrian, the artist's translation of his conflicts "from symbol to sign" meant that he relegated art to "a mode of moral etiquette."[16] Art historian Peter Bürger has launched a similar missile at the twentieth-century avant-garde, arguing that in modernism and twentieth-century art generally, art lost any political edge as it became increasingly self-referential and increasingly cordoned off from the politics of everyday life.[17] The translation of perversion, neurosis, social conflict, and artistic rebellion into self-referential art—into *gallery art*—may just work to strip art of the possibility of social meaning, of its potential as "disturbatory." The links between aesthetics and decorousness, between sublimation and the social niceties, might be construed, from certain political vantage points, as an argument for pornography over art.

If the categorical distinctions between art and pornography come down to issues of sublimation, including the class imperatives to produce it, the problem with pornography is simply its failure to translate one set of contents into another. The problem seems to be that it produces a body of images that are too *blatantly* out of the unconscious, too *unaesthetically* written in the language of obsession, compulsion, perversion, infantile desires, rage, fear, pain, and misogyny. Too literally about sex and power rather than their aesthetically coded forms, as in the works of any number of well-respected artists and writers whose work dwells on similar themes. Too *potent* for art.

As the distinctions between art and perversion begin to unravel, perhaps some of the certainty about what pornography is unravels also. This isn't necessarily an argument for moving pornography into the art galleries and museums. Aesthetics may rely on perversity, perversity may be aesthetically complex, but sublimation isn't imaginary: the pornographic response is still viscerally and experientially distinct from the aesthetic response.

This *is* an argument, however, for regarding pornography (when we regard it theoretically, and as a social practice) similarly to the way we regard artistic production, rather than as a distinct and completely unrelated enterprise. It's also an argument for applying the same degree of critical, interpretive acumen to pornography as we do to art, for understanding porn as imbued with theatrical and semiotic complexity, with nuance and social meaning. (Perhaps this sort of understanding would have led to a different outcome in the DePew case.) It's not only a naked woman, it's not just a pair of lace panties, it's a condensation of narratives of the entry into the social order, the passage from infancy to childhood to adulthood, the prisonhouse of binary gender-role assignment, of mother- dominated childrearing, *and* the oppression of women. But as Louise Kaplan indicates, the woman in the porn pictorial is just as likely to represent the female longings of the male viewer he wants to subjugate as it is to express, in some literal way, his desire to oppress me. There's no reason to assume that pornographic images function any more literally (or produce more literal effects) than other more socially elevated images that we're accustomed to reading for their symbolic and latent meanings—no reason other than class prejudice against "working photographs" or pure censoriousness against sexual pleasure.

Then what stops us from looking as closely at transvestite self-portraiture as the art-critical establishment does at Cindy Sherman's work, or as an art historian examining the self-portrait of a little-known period painter? What stops us from searching within these forms also, for clues about how this artist experiences himself within a specific social, moral, and psychological context? Like the self-portrait throughout history, these portraits too contain a multitude of detail about the subject's particular milieu and its mores.

* * *

Let's try looking beyond the bodies, at the *mise-en-scènes* of these transvestite self-portraits. Most often the subject chooses to pose himself in his domestic space, affording the viewer a voyeuristic glimpse into his home decor and environs. The juxtapositions of the body and its social geography condenses, in tableau, the lived experience of gendered contradiction. For quite often these tableaus are familial ones. Surrounding the bodies in pornography are narratives: for example, the suburban melodrama set in the neat and decorous living room. The interior design, by an unseen wifely hand, says marriage, affluence, subterfuge. This isn't the East Village: this is clearly a place where gender codes are so punitively enforced that being exposed transgressing them—"Dad's wearing a dress!"—would mean humiliation, disgrace, and scandal. Viewing these photos, we're forced on to intimate terms with small-scale social tyranny, with the burdens of secrecy and shame. These are the kinds of narratives that are so easy to disregard, if you—firmly wedged into your assigned, "normal" gender-binary—smugly assume yourself to fall outside the policing of everyday life.

These self-portraits are very much dramas of the domestic. Living rooms and bedrooms are both popular settings, but a number of men choose to pose themselves in their kitchens—because it's the most feminine space in the house? The image of a glamourous yet virile blond in four-inch heels perched seductively on the kitchen counter—the shiny kitchen appliances, dish soap, cute spice rack, and harvest-motif wallpaper competing visually with her erect penis—suggests the American sitcom suburban mom as imagined by suburban surrealist David Lynch. It suggests the absent presence of a "real" wife, as well, with the kitchen as gendered turf conveying something about the ways that both the wife we see and the wives we don't are equally padlocked into social gender stereotypes and their assigned domestic spaces. The wife-impersonator, gazing impudently into the camera, usurping the "rightful" occupant (and *her* narrative), verifies the complaints of many TV wives that their husbands are competitive as women: spending more time on looks, more money on clothes, making the wives feel dumpy and inferior as women. (Feminists have often expressed resentment of the fact that the transvestite male may foray into femininity, but he in no way relinquishes any of the prerogatives of male power. Thus transvestism has been of a certain ambivalent interest to feminist theorists of gender: on the one hand there's the sense of an alliance with the project of challenging traditional gender roles; on the other, the suspicion that these guys are just caricaturing the "worst" aspects of femininity and are, deep down, quite hostile to women.[18])

The juxtaposition of a beefy man in baby doll lingerie pouting into the camera, posed in front of a Swedish modern breakfront displaying a neatly arranged collection of Time-Life books and china figurines—with a wedding photo in the background—says everything about carefully compartmentalized secrets and the fantasy of seamless "normal" surfaces, with this insistent display of all the props and set pieces of happy American home life. It's an image that almost makes you understand the popularity of national leaders like Ronald Reagan or national fantasies like the Contract with America—both devoted to carefully constructed, overproduced surfaces, to cynical (and completely fictive, at least according to Reagan daughter Patti) promises of sitcom family normalcy, of docile mothers and strong fathers who will bomb us out of perversity and back to God-given sex roles and their respective, separate, wardrobes.

Sometimes the self-portraitist will send in not just one photo, but an entire layout, posing himself in every room of the house and affording you the honored guest's guided tour: the formal dining room, the rec room with the CD collection and component stereo system, the master bedroom suite. As is conventional throughout the history of portraiture, he pictorially surrounds himself with his property and possessions. What mute appeal is being issued here? Schooled by the influential art historian John Berger in "ways of seeing" early oil paintings, we're alerted that these objects supply us with information about the poser's position in the world—his class status and material wealth, obviously—but also about what *possession* itself implies: entitlement, citizenship, the assertion of a right.[19] Given what we know about the disdain heaped on the male transvestite in our society, this self-protective gathering of one's possessions around oneself seems ironically, or sadly, talismanic. (According to Berger, pictorial qualities such as these are gendered: a man's presence is dependent on displayed forms of external power and possessions, whereas a woman's presence is in her physical appearance. Transvestite self-portraits, not surprisingly, walk right down the middle.)

The more of these photos I looked at, the more curious I became about why so many transvestites seem to have matching bedspreads and curtains in their bedrooms. Had I stumbled onto the missing link in the etiology of transvestism through my close reading of transvestite home decor? Something about matching fabric?

I finally realized that what I was looking at were motel rooms. There's something both banal and tragic about the implication of these photos: unacceptable sartorial desires that the protagonist has managed to keep hidden from a wife and family. Here's a brief window on to what it's like to be unable to reveal the most central thing about yourself to your partner in life. Is there anyone who can't imagine the catastrophe that exposure would mean in a life carefully constructed around a sexual secret, and feel the small stab of fear (or maybe even a tiny bit of pleasure) at the havoc that would ensue? Is there anyone who hasn't at one time had a shameful secret? Here *is* a universal drama for you.

One thing to add about this evident sexual secrecy is that, once again, it flies in the face of the clinical literature, specifically Robert Stoller's account of the essential role of women in the causation and maintenance of transvestism. According to Stoller, who has written extensively about transvestites and transsexuals, "The women of transvestites . . . all share the attribute of taking a conscious and intense pleasure in seeing males dressed as females. All have in common a fear of and a need to ruin masculinity." The cooperation of women is essential for "'successful' transvestism," and the fact that some men are able to pass as women is "almost invariably due" to wives and girlfriends—"succorers," Stoller calls them—who, because of their own concealed rage at men, devote themselves to teaching the transvestite how to dress, walk, and use makeup.[20] Stoller, of course, has much to say about mothers as well. When in doubt, pin the blame on a woman.

Having somewhat briefly considered these transvestite self-portraits from the vantage point of our hypothetical art historian, we can now place them within their social context. So consider, alongside transvestite pornography, all the nervous jokes floating around the culture about discovering a man in women's clothes, and consider, alongside those, all the examples of popular comedy and popular culture that contrive, through elaborate and improbable means, to put men in women's clothes—from *Some Like It Hot* to *Tootsie* to *Mrs. Doubtfire*, to fraternity rituals, comedy revues, and so on. There's clearly a vast cultural anxiety around cross-dressing, coexisting with an equally vast fascination about the transgression of the codes of proper dress for the proper sex.[21] And hovering somewhere in the vicinity of all this anxious comedy is an uneasy recognition of the casual everyday violence that enforces those clothing edicts, the queasy knowledge that when social conditioning fails, these conventions of "normal" dress are enforced by coercion, threat of the law, and emotional blackmail. You're always just a sartorial slip—or getting caught in your wife's slip—away from cultural exile, from becoming the neighborhood joke.

And what about the suburban husband who finds—for whatever buried reason—his deepest desires out of step with his culture's expectations of them? It's from this kind of narrative that mainstream culture prefers to avert its gaze. Although we flock to high-culture spectacles (theater, opera) full of tragedy and pathos, are ever compelled by classic motifs like the hero whose fatal flaw becomes his undoing or the protagonist persecuted and misunderstood in his own time, we're most reluctant to recognize not only the way similar motifs are expressed within pornography—within "low culture"—but how intimately pornography is linked to these same cultural preoccupations.

In reading all pornography more closely, we might uncover other histories, other narratives, perhaps crudely written, and perhaps, as Louise Kaplan says of perverse scenarios, exposing one thing to distract you from thinking about another. The perverse strategy hides through exposure, working overtime to deflect your attention from what's really at stake. Pornography exposes a lot of naked bodies, but sometimes as camouflage and diversion. Often what looks like power are props, compensatory mechanisms, and empty signifiers. In insisting—as do antiporn feminists—that pornography is transparently about male erections and female disempowerment, what remains hidden? In insisting that art and pornography are two completely separate enterprises, what meanings do we risk missing?

The repetition that characterizes all pornography, the compulsive return to the same scenarios and scripts, have the driven character that's the mark of material emanating from the unconscious. But certainly this is also true of what we designate art—

in fact, one of the unstated requirements to *be* an artist is the ability to construct a consistent body of work, one unified exactly by marks of repetition, the obsession with particular themes, by recurrent, recognizable yearnings and unmastered compulsions. (If you've mastered them, why bother to paint them?)

Aesthetics are crucial to who we are as selves and what we are as a culture. Taste, delicacy, beauty, manners, and social conventions—all of which pornography sets itself the task of energetically violating—constitute the aesthetic. But rather than some timeless, elevated, high-minded thing, aesthetics are historically specific, completely class bound, racialized, and often, in fact, vindictively cruel to who and what falls outside its quite capricious dictates: whether those problematic nonbinary genders (as we've seen) or those problematic nonconforming bodies (as we're about to see). Pornography devotes itself to thwarting aesthetic conventions wherever and whenever it can, to disrupting our precious sensibilities at every turn. It's the antiaesthetic. This is a social undertaking not without philosophical and political significance.

The repetitions in transvestite pornography are affixed to something quite universal, which is the history that all gendered subjects share, and from which some of us have emerged more unscathed than others. Pornography, like other kinds of expressive culture, is a place that these submerged narratives are unveiled. But probably here, more so than in polite culture—that is, more than in those versions of culture willing to relegate themselves to forms of "moral etiquette"—you have to be willing to squint, appraise, discern, turn it on its side, and then not run screaming from the room when, in response, it kicks you where it hurts: in your aesthetics.

Three

Life in the
Fat Lane

Fat. Few topics excite as much interest, emotion, or capital investment. With a multi-billion-dollar diet and fitness industry, tens of millions of joggers, bikers, and power walkers out on any sunny weekend all trying to banish fat, work off fat, atone for fat, health ideologues who talk of little these days besides fat, research and development dollars working overtime to invent no-fat substitutes for fat—our intense wish for fat's absence is just what ensures its cultural omnipresence.

Fat is the theme of our new national literature; its drama never ceases to compel us, to hold us in its thrall. A book on measuring fat spent over three years on the *New York Times* best-seller list: no other subject can so reliably incite Americans to actually read. The novel may be floundering, but the war on fat (like so many of our previous wars) is rich with literary possibilities: a heroic, epic, tragically doomed battle waged by a front line of diet strategists and tacticians, armed with the latest physiological intelligence (monounsaturates, good cholesterol, high carbohydrates), and backed up by a phalanx of psychologists on the home front, bent on putting fat on the couch and interpreting its deeper meanings (it's your anger, your fear of sex, your hatred of your mother, your needy inner child).

Given the vast quantities of energy and resources devoted to annihilating it, and, in turn, making life miserable for those who are unfortunate enough to bear the humiliation of its exposure, fat might be considered not just an obsessive focus, but perhaps the crux of contemporary American culture. The mission of all this cultural energy? To ensure fat's invisibility and exterminate it from public view.

So perhaps this explains the existence of a genre of pornography whose entire purpose is to *expose* fat. If one aspect of pornography's social function is to provide a repository for those threatening, problematic materials and imagery banished from the culture at large—for the *unaesthetic*—then the brazen appearance of fat within the refuge of the porn store has a certain inevitability. And appear it does, in an array of magazines and videos featuring extremely large naked women in sexual situations (by large I mean between maybe two hundred and five hundred pounds), with titles like *Plumpers and Big Women, Jumbo Jezebel, Life in the Fat Lane,* and *Love's Savage Cupcake.* Or for gay men, there's *Bulk Male, Husky,* and *Bustin Apart at the Seams.* Too bad for the interests of politesse that these loathsome eyesores we try and try again to deport from sight don't seem content to be shunted off to their visual leper colonies, never to be heard from again. Instead they're continually circling the perimeter, waiting for the right moment to break back in. The fact that so many pornographic subgenres are so strikingly contiguous with the central aesthetic preoccupations of our day—like fat—means that the aesthetic has to be forever vigilant against these threatened incursions from all the banished contents, and from the unsightly classes, and vigilant against the profound unsettling they do to our sensibilities.

That fat might contain erotic charge in a culture so maniacally devoted to achieving thinness that vomiting food is a national epidemic among college women makes either no sense or perfect sense, depending on how you understand the relation between sexuality and the larger social context. If our culture demands svelte, toned, bulgeless bodies, does it immediately follow that everyone's sexual preferences fall obediently into line? Perhaps, perhaps not.

But are those sexual nonconformists whose desires fall outside the bounds of current bodily fashion automatically deserving of the damning label "fetishist"? (Even the porn industry labels fat porn "fetish material," although perhaps with less scorn, and less *medicalization*, then the culture at large.) But if you stop and think about it, what really separates a preference for fat bodies from those "normal" fetishes, like a preference for in-shape bodies with buns of steel (on men and women), or for breasts (big ones, please), or washboard abs— other than prevailing fashion? And of course, one need never visit a porn store to get one's visual fill of thin bodies—they're on constant display *everywhere* for your visual enjoyment and your private fantasies. Yet whither fat? Hiding under that shapeless *shmata,* or behind the closed doors of that Weight Watchers meeting, or on the "before" side of some promised miraculous transformation. Or in pornography.

Isn't fat always sort of pornographic anyway? Because interestingly, even a magazine like *Dimensions,* whose visuals are far tamer than *Playboy* or *Penthouse* (its pictorials are all very large models posed in lingerie), is available only in hard-core porn stores or by mail. *Dimensions,* a magazine "where big is beautiful," is aimed at what are termed "fat admirers," that is, men who prefer fat female sex partners. But *Dimensions* is written in the idiom of social activism; its primary topic is social discrimination against fat admiration. *Dimensions* is on the side of discretion (the lingeried body) and taste (no dirty jokes here), yet it happens that its taste is for fat; thus, into the pornography racks it goes, because fat, it seems, is pornographic in and of itself. Given this close kinship between fat and pornography, delving into the social relations of fat may give us some backdoor insights into what's at risk for dominant culture in the pornographic enterprise.

Fat is a site of deep social contradiction. Fat is something a significant percentage of the American public bears not only undisguised contempt for, but also in many cases, an intense, unexamined, visceral disgust. (And although I'm writing about norms within white America, minority cultures are hardly exempt from the bodily ideals peddled by the dominant culture.)

Here, a trained psychiatrist writes of the feelings of repugnance stirred in him by a fat woman patient he calls Betty:

> I have always been repelled by fat women. I find them disgusting: their absurd sidewise waddle, their absence of body contour—breasts, laps, buttocks, shoulders, jawlines, cheekbones, *everything*, everything I like to see in a woman, obscured in an avalanche of flesh. And I hate their clothes —the shapeless, baggy dresses or, worse, the stiff elephantine blue jeans with the barrel thighs. How dare they impose that body on the rest of us?

"The origins of these sorry feelings?" he wonders. The answer: "I had never thought to inquire"—although the patient who hits this nerve does provide the psychiatrist (also a professor at Stanford) the opportunity to work through what he calls "a great trial of counter-transference."[1] This particular fat-hating shrink is hardly alone in his undertheorized anxiety: according to fat activists, fat hatred is more or less demanded by the culture, not to mention the last remaining protectorate of safe bigotry.[2] A recent *New England Journal of Medicine* study claiming to be the first "to document the profound social and economic consequences of obesity" merely confirms what any fat person will tell you—that this culture treats the fat population with an unparalleled viciousness.[3]

What's remarkable is how little general cultural explanation there is for this national revulsion toward fat. As everyone who's cruised the psychology section of any bookstore is aware, there's an expanding body of literature now devoted to the devastating effects of the cult of thinness on women's lives, generally pointing a blaming finger at the media and fashion industries. There's a fairly vast literature—clinical, popular, literary—on anorexia and bulimia, and a corresponding expansion of metaphor around the vicious cycle of food deprivation and overconsumption. All the metaphors suggested by these titles point to a psychology of neediness: *The Famine Within, The Hungry Self, Starving for Attention, Feeding the Empty Heart, Feeding the Hungry Heart,* etc. Most of us can knowledgeably speculate about why it is people, most often women, voluntarily starve themselves: at the level of individual psychology, any eating-disorder cognoscenti will tell you it's about mothers and control issues; turning to social psychology, you'll find feminist indictments of society's desire to diminish women, particularly now that women are achieving more social power and visibility. Intellectuals have provided us with sophisticated analyses of cultural ambivalence about the maternal body, and even geopolitical insights about what it might mean to refuse food in a society devoted to overconsumption. Philosophers have speculated about what thinness means in our social cosmology: thinness speaks for the self, it embodies aspirations around the control of impulses and regulation of desires in a society that encourages us to lose control at the sight of desirable commodities: the slender body signals a well-managed self.[4] But there's surprisingly little attention devoted to just what it is about fat qua fat that's so very disturbing at this particular historical moment, and to what could account for the intense, visceral repulsion it provokes. It seems, actually, like a fairly stupid question.

One reason the question seems so stupid is the appearance of nature and common sense that attach themselves to this anxiety and repulsion about fat. Fat is simply unaesthetic. If pressed we resort to medical explanations. "It's not healthy to be fat," we proclaim knowledgeably as we reach for the little pink envelope of chemical compounds known to cause fatal diseases in lab rats, or as we ingest glutinous and ill-conceived oxymorons like nonfat desserts. And current medical ideology works overtime reinforcing this common sense. I say "medical ideology" to make a stab at stripping away some of its pretense to scientific certainty. In fact, the visual taste for thinness—fairly hegemonic since the end of World War I—far preceded current medical notions about fat: medical ideology followed fashion rather than vice versa.[5] But even though there's a preponderance of evidence that weight and distribution of body fat are for the most part genetically determined—including a recent National Institutes of Health study that concluded "There is increasing physiological, biochemical and genetic evidence that overweight is not a simple disorder of will power, as is sometimes implied, but is a complex disorder of energy metabolism"— this has had little effect on the medical establishment's insistence on low ideal body weights or the guilt trips it imposes on the fat population.

Neither have these sorts of genetic conclusions had any impact on the larger culture's fat phobia, which according to anecdotal accounts by fat people, doctors overwhelmingly share. Fat activists point out that any oppressed population suffers from stress-related illness, as witness the well-documented incidence of high blood pressure among African-Americans. The reliance on medical explanations for fat loathing hardly seems to account for the intensity of the experience and is rather, I suspect, part of the symptomatology, rather than its source. Particularly if you consider that smokers or drinkers are generally treated with mild disapproval at worst—certainly nothing near the full-fledged contempt reserved for the fat.

This cult of bodily thinness and obsession with banishing fat is, of course, historically recent, and in sharp contrast to bodily aesthetics for the past four hundred years or so. Between roughly 1500 and 1900, a hefty body was a visually appealing body, for both men and women. Paintings throughout the period portray both sexes as solid and even rotund. Nudes—à la Rubens— shamelessly displayed thick pink rolls of flesh. And clothes themselves were bulky and designed to add volume to the body rather than emphasize a svelte profile. If you were thin you did your best to hide it under large, bunchy garments.

That body types had complicated social connotations is a fairly unproblematic insight when thinking art historically. In Rubens' time, for example, thinness had largely negative connotations of poverty and deprivation, along with the insinuation of disease and old age. Being thin implied something dark and suspicious about the person's inner being as well: a spiritual poverty or moral insufficiency. The thin lacked good fortune, not to mention will and zest: thinness connoted morbidity, a lack of life. Previously, in the Middle Ages, thinness had been considered aesthetically pleasing, given the way it echoed the Church's teaching on the unimportance of the flesh. But by the time Rubens came along, an emerging humanism, represented in the Renaissance faith in the limitless possibilities of the human mind and body, was expressed visually in depictions of bodies of weight and rotund sensuousness, with the full, solid body expressing a sense of social stability and order.[6]

So what will the art historians of the next century have to say about late-twentieth-century bodily norms and fashions? What will they make of our particular mode of depicting bodies, including the photographic record? After all, there are a range of body types in the culture, and if only one type is typically represented—in our advertisements, movies, TV—this type, as with depictions of bodily largeness in Rubens' day, must certainly reveal something about our social preoccupations. What connections between socially sanctioned bodies and social ideologies will become obvious?

One fairly clear link between the body and the social is the complex chain of association between body type and social class. More or less since the beginning of the century, thinness began to be affiliated with wealth and higher social standing, whereas fatness now tends to be associated both stereotypically *and* factually with the lower classes. (And of course everyone knows the duchess of Windsor's adage—the one that inspired three generations of upwardly mobile anorexics with its assertion that you can never be too rich or too thin.)

There is, in fact, a higher concentration of body fat the lower down the income scale you go in this country. According to the National Center for Health Statistics, almost 30 percent of women with incomes below $10,000 a year are obese, as compared with 12.7 percent of those with incomes above $50,000 a year.[7] But interestingly, all the clichés—that fat is more tolerated farther down the social ladder, or that there's a greater consumption of pork rinds and doughnuts—are not so much the case as that fat is actually a predictor of downward mobility: if fat, you have a lower chance of being hired, and if hired a lower chance of being promoted. And this is particularly true in jobs with a greater concentration of women—sales, secretarial, flight attendants—jobs where appearance, whether acknowledged or not, is often one of the criteria in hiring and promotion. Heterosexual fat women are less likely to marry "up" socially or economically. And given that the tendency to fat is inherited, fat children are more likely to be born into a lower social class and because of fat discrimination, to stay there.[8]

This association between fat and the lower classes is yet another twist in the twisted tale of current social responses to fat. Fat seems to carry a certain imaginary narrative with it, an origins tale of how the fat person got to be that way, the shameful revelation of clandestine (or overt) gluttony and overconsumption. But in class terms this has to be seen as something of a displacement: it assigns responsibility for overconsumption and gluttony to the social class by far least culpable of overconsuming. Researchers studying the psychology of body image report that fat is associated with a range of fears: from loss of control to a reversion to infantile desires, to failure, self-loathing, sloth, and passivity. Substitute "welfare class" for "fat" here and you start to see that the phobia of fat and the phobia of the poor are heavily cross-coded, and that perhaps the fear of an out-of-control body is not unrelated to the fear of out-of-control masses with their voracious demands and insatiable appetites—not just for food, but for social resources and entitlement programs. In fact, linking the poor to fat is now an explicit tactic in Republican aspirations to cut welfare: as Republican presidential hopeful Phil Gramm told a Texas audience—referring to a Dallas newspaper's article about a family rationing food to avoid hunger—"Did you see the picture? Here are these people who are skimping to avoid hunger, and they are all fat!" Laughing, he continued, "Because of the impact of food stamps where we force people to buy food when, given a choice, they would choose to spend the aid we give them on other things, we're the only nation in the world where all our poor people are fat."[9] Clearly if the poor would only agree to diet, we could get rid of that pesky national deficit. (And now it becomes clear that Clinton's New Democrat enthusiasm for slashing welfare can be read as something of a reaction-formation to his own weight-control problems.)

How could consumption issues *not* provoke the most anxious and ambivalent responses about the control of desire and appetite—given a society that on the one hand deeply wishes us to overconsume, yet savagely punishes all bodily evidence of such? And a society that also, somewhat illogically, links such bodily testaments of consumption (namely fat) to various forms of failure: to sexual failure (not being "attractive enough"), the failure to be a proper consumer (the connotations of lower-classness), and general all-round social failure (the fat pariah). Control of the body, desire, and appetite are qualities historically associated with the bourgeoisie and their social triumph: fat both signifies loss of self mastery, but also threatens loss of the class status for which bodily self-control is a prerequisite.

The fat are seen to be violating territorial limits: they take up too much room, too many resources (much like our nation—and internationally, extreme obesity is seen as a peculiarly American disorder). But why is it that fat stands in so well for all forms of overconsuming; why is fat so mocked and ridiculed when other spectacles of overconsumption, like TV producer Aaron Spelling's ridiculously bloated $50-million, 52,503-square-foot, 123-room Beverly Hills mansion (with an entire room devoted to gift-wrapping packages for wife, Candy), earns him instead a layout in *Vanity Fair*? Fat is by far the only physical characteristic so deeply culturally connotative. The burden borne by the fat is not only of pounds, it's the sorry fate of being trapped in a body that conveys such an excess of meanings.

One of the best accounts of the social experience of being fat is a book called *Such a Pretty Face*.[10] The title derives from what seems to be a universal experience of fat women: hearing this sanctimonious one-liner delivered by everyone from "well-meaning" relatives to (in startling violation of norms of social conduct) strangers on the street or in restaurants. What the line, of course, means is "if *only* you'd lose weight." But what puts the public on such terms of immediate intimacy with the fat? Fat people report that it's very common to have pig noises directed at them when they walk down the street. Other types of public ridicule are common. One fat woman tells of attending a college lecture with over a hundred people in it. The professor stops speaking in the middle of a sentence and says to her, "When are you going to lose weight? You're really fat."[11] What makes the fat a kind of public property whose bodies invite the vocal speculations and ridicule of strangers? And why are these verbal assaults so often prescriptive, so dedicated to the project of inducing the fat to thinness? What imaginative investment does our citizenry have in putting the fat on diets?

Of course the individual body in American culture is pretty much the sole locale for scenarios of transformation: you can aerobicize it, liposuction it, contract it through diet or expand selected parts with collagen injections. A fat person seems to be regarded as a transformation waiting to happen, a vast virgin American frontier onto which can be projected the transformative fantasies of the culture at large. Maybe the scandal of fatness is its insult to those collective transformative fantasies, the affront of a body that dares to remain fat and untransformed. But of course the real scandal is that this utopian investment in potential social transformation is, when displaced to the individual body, both fantasmatic and doomed to fail: the recidivism rate for dieters is estimated at 98 percent. Although there must be some disavowed level of awareness on the part of the public that to be fat is largely beyond individual control, at the same time the culture's deeply held belief is that the fat could change but have *chosen* not to. Whereas the experience of being

103

fat is that of wanting to change but not being able to. This transformational incapacity is the basis of the fabulous success of the diet industry, and what makes it a perfect investment opportunity.

The angry, contemptuous social reaction to the resistance of the fat to refashioning themselves is a testament to the very degree of our investment in the potential for change. The reaction toward this spectacle of stasis is, in many cases, actual violence: 25 percent of fat men and 16 percent of fat women reported being hit or threatened with physical violence because of their weight. And emotional violence is nearly universal: 90 percent of fat people surveyed report incidents of derision, ridicule, contempt, and scorn on account of their weight.[12]

But what fat also conjures up is the terrifying specter of an insatiability that all we social citizens have, to varying degrees, learned to suppress. Fat advertises "naked need," need that surpasses the ability of the available resources—whether edible, monetary, or emotional—to quell it. A fat person is a one-body smash-and-grab riot: like that anarchic rebellious moment when social controls fail and you take what you want, when you want it, without regard for proprieties like ownership, or eat all you want, without regard for consequences, like obesity. The spectacle of fat, and the bedlam of free-form consumption the nonfat imagine as its origin, excites those same longings for plenitude (and equal distribution of it) that factor into our simultaneous fascination and hatred for the rich. Can it be coincidental that the best slogan for socialism is "Eat the rich," given that consumption is the everyday negotiation between need, desire, and resources—which always exists in combination with a wary, jealous watchfulness about who's getting the "bigger piece of the pie"?

The issue of "choice" seems central to the fat problem. Fat activists have seized on evidence provided by recent genetic research indicating that the propensity for fat is genetic, deploying it as conclusive evidence of fat oppression and social victimization. Their argument is that if fat is no more chosen than say, race, bigotry toward the fat should be no more officially sanctioned than racism—and activists hope that these new findings will result in institutional recourse like their own Title 7 act. (Only one state—Michigan—currently has laws forbidding employment discrimination on the basis of size.) Activists are now able to claim confidently that the fat glutton is a vicious stereotype and that the fat often actually eat less than the thin; being fat, they say, has nothing to do with food or caloric intake but is a metabolic disorder. You find very little in fat-activist literature that goes so far as to endorse choosing to be fat: the fat person is generally cast in the role of the victim (although often an angry victim) rather than the role of the defiant. It's something that's been foisted upon you by your metabolism, rather than something for which you bear culpability.

This back and forth over personal responsibility for socially marginal or reviled traits resonates interestingly with the recent controversial and much discussed findings by a researcher at the National Cancer Institute indicating a genetic basis for homosexuality—evidence that links male homosexuality to a particular region of the X chromosome. This discovery led to speculation in the mainstream press that this would be the great leap forward for more widespread social acceptance of homosexuality: after all, the argument seemed to go, if you don't choose to be gay but are "born that way," then there really is little grounds for discrimination. (Which, of course, seems remarkably forgetful about the experience of racial minorities in this country.)

Coincidentally, the discovery of the "gay gene" comes along just as one wing of the gay community has appropriated the formerly derogatory label "queer" as the badge for a new kind of political activism, and just as AIDS activists, too, are insisting that issues surrounding sexual object choice—and the public-health issues that overlap with sexuality—are political. Proponents of queer politics make a distinction between being gay and being queer: to follow the genetic analogy, you might be born gay but you *choose* to be queer—being queer is a political act. So rather than groveling for the straight majority's understanding and beneficence to remedy intolerance, queer activists announce, "We're here, we're queer, get used to it." And the successes of AIDS activist groups like ACT UP in pushing through reforms in the way government and the scientific community are dealing with the AIDS crisis suggests there are alternatives to politeness or playing the victim or waiting around for tolerance and understanding.

Fat-activist literature, on the other hand—to continue the analogy—has tended to take the genetic "born-that-way" line, as opposed to the "choosing to be queer" position. Until very recently there's been little stomach for choosing to defy social bodily norms along the lines of a queer politics. The preference among an earlier generation of fat activists—and perhaps in reaction to the general cultural insistence on individual blame for fatness—had been to regard fat as nonvolitional and to demand the majority's understanding, as opposed to an in-your-face defiance of social bodily controls. Recently though, younger, angrier fat women have spawned a number of fat "zines"—small, homemade, cheaply and independently published magazines that import a queer sensibility to the issue of fat. Zines like *Fat!So?*, "For people who don't apologize for their size," and *Fat Girl*, "A Zine for Fat Dykes and the Women Who Want Them," take a more mutinous tone than the earlier generation's lamentations about social prejudice.

But still, while much of the political wing of the gay community reacted with suspicion to the news of the "gay gene," protesting that whenever there's a new "cause" for homosexuality proposed, there shortly follow proposed "cures,"[13] there isn't the same zeal to preserve fat against elimination. Certainly there are extensive protests against the dangers of specific fat cures, like surgery, which risks death for thinness, and against the insistence on diets, because diets don't work, but in general you'd have to search long and hard to find anyone who, given a choice, would choose a fat body. It may be the case that there's even greater discrimination against fat than against homosexuality, and with none of the same pleasures or rewards; there isn't a comparable fat subculture (no bars, no parades, no landmark events to rally around like Stonewall), although one organization, NAAFA (National Association to Advance Fat Acceptance) does have an annual convention and local social events. Instead of fat subculture, there's the diet industry, and the ever-present, inescapable conversational din about calories, grapefruits, fat grams, and the five pounds you gained on vacation, which provides the aural backdrop of American culture at the tail end of the twentieth century, and all of which means the death knell to fat. Regardless of who suffers the "most" discrimination, queers or the fat, the experience of being fat in this culture is so devastating that a majority of those who have lost weight through surgery report that they would rather lose a limb, or for many even eyesight, than be fat again, which is some testimony to the degree of paralyzing, devastating cultural hatred that fat citizens endure, although less and less silently.

The escalating anger and defiance level of fat activists may be partly due to the influence of queer politics, which is very much in the air these days. But it's also the case that all categories of social victimization are lately fueled by intensified anger and increasing demands for public forums to air a snowballing assortment of social grievances. It's easy enough to feel contemptuous and superior to the latest round of daytime talk show guests and their snivelings, as does critic Robert Hughes in his best seller *Culture of Complaint,* a book that was widely hailed as the long-awaited chewing-out that the whining classes deserved.[14] But it's also the case that one of the only ways that individuals can enter political discourse these days is under the rubric of The Victim, and it's important to understand how these victim claims displace political demands from the realm of politics to the realm of culture. Which is exactly why making overly facile and overly rigid distinctions between culture and politics, as Hughes does, leads to trivializing and misunderstanding popular culture *and* its audiences, as Hughes also does. The complaint is a form that often condenses contents that are socially significant, but which have no other access to language or intelligibility.[15] Fat itself can function as just this sort of complaint—not only an individual foible, not only a bodily symptom, but a form of social articulation. And this may also have something to do with the hostility to which it's routinely subjected.

This is the question that was taken up on a 1994 episode of "The Jerry Springer Show" (a daytime talk show) whose ostensible subject was "Fat Greeting Cards." In case you haven't strolled down the greeting card aisle lately, the once-harmless greeting card has evolved into a semipornographic cultural form of free-floating grossness, hostility, and general obscenity rivaling *Hustler* magazine (and here too, the fart joke is king). Whether this is a natural reaction to the reign of Hallmark-style bathos and sentimentality, or simply the most logical form with which to express the human propensity for ambivalence in social relationships ("Happy Birthday and here's a fart joke to help you celebrate") is difficult to know. In any case, given the greeting card's new preoccupation with the improper, needless to say, fat jokes, fat humor, and fat bodies also abound. These fat greeting cards feature corpulent, naked, or seminude men or women, usually paired with some correspondingly witless caption: "Every inch a lady" or "The first time I saw you in tight jeans . . . I knew you weren't just another pretty face." A four-hundred-pound "bride" announces, "I heard you're getting married. . . . You must be *bursting* with joy." The women are garbed in lingerie, or sometimes nude, heavily made up, and shown in sexualized poses, wearing seductive expressions. The cards featuring men follow the naturist motif of fat male porn: a male "teddy bear" is posed in the woods, nude except for a strategically placed scratch-away applique with the message "Scratch away my fig leaf and find out what nature has for you!"

The "Fat Greeting Cards" debate featured a panel of fat women greeting card models (300 to 525 pounds) on one side of the issue, with most of the audience and host Jerry Springer on the other. The fat women took the position that they liked posing for the cards. For them, it's a source of self-esteem, income, sexual possibilities, and even a form of revenge. Susan: "People have been looking at me, staring, pointing all my life. Now they have to pay two bucks for the privilege."[16]

Springer's audience, on the other hand, had nothing but contempt for these fat women greeting card models, with Springer taking the paternalistic position that the women were exposing themselves to ridicule and laughter and somehow weren't aware of it. For Springer it was inevitable that a fat body could invite only one response: mockery. This despite the fact that the models insisted that posing for the cards made them feel glamourous, sexy, and positive about their bodies.

Springer: "How does it feel knowing that people are going into these—into the grocery stores, supermarkets, card shops— they're looking at that, and you know, a lot of them are laughing?" Ambrosia, one of the fat models, answers, "Well, that's their problem. That's not mine." The women say fat-affirmative things like "Beauty comes in all sizes, and this is my size." Jean adds, "I enjoy doing it too."

This is too much for Springer. "What about the idea that people may be—that they look at you as a caricature of a fat person?" Susan however, insists, "This is an issue of control. We've taken control here. This is something that we choose to do with our bodies and our images, and no one has the right to tell us not to do it." An audience member counters, "This is not a positive image for women of size. . . . You're perpetrating the lie that fat women are not attractive by doing this." Jean rightly points out, "But it's *you* saying that we're not attractive. There's nothing unattractive about me!" One of the (female) audience members tells one of the panelists to get a shorter set of pearls "because they're sticking between your boobs there, and it's making me ill." Another (female) audience member accuses the panelists of being "starved for attention." Springer insists, speaking for womenkind at large, "What [women watching the show at home] worry about is this card perpetuates all these fat jokes in our society" and adds, somewhat illogically, "There are a lot of fat women out there who now have more people making fun of them because we continue to make fun of people who are fat."

The question valiantly trying to surface here is whether the cards make fat women into grotesques. Clearly what opens these women to ridicule—or this is Springer's worry—is that they're sexualized, that they're appearing in exactly the kind of lingerie and heavy makeup that any universal sex symbol—say, Madonna —would. Springer ends the show on a sanctimonious note that once again fails the test of logic: "The image being fostered here is one that tends to ridicule or negatively stereotype fat people. Let's be honest. Men who buy these cards aren't doing it to get turned on, though our guests today certainly could turn men on. No, these cards are being bought to make fat jokes . . . let's not pretend that people aren't being hurt here." Springer seems under the impression that fat greeting cards invented abusiveness toward the fat.

If the "Fat Greeting Cards" show indicates something about the frenzy of hostility and illogic that the unapologetic appearance of fat leaves in its wake, it also indicates fat's transgressive virtuosity. Springer, befuddled by these defiantly fat women, dedicates himself to the project of protecting fat women from ridicule (including his own) by forcing fat back into the closet. Women in the audience were dedicated to the project of expressing their rage at other women who dared to thumb their noses at female size norms. It's clear that the unapologetic exposure of fat provokes the most savage forms of policing, with the citizenry transforming itself into a private militia dedicated to squelching the potential insurrection naked fat somehow seems to threaten—at least to the twentieth-century psyche.

Fat is not an uncomplicated affair. Neither are talk show debates, or pornography, or other forms of low culture. Neither is the complaint itself. What does it mean when a cultural critic dedicates himself to telling us that things are simple, and spins a best seller out of a shopworn platitude like "No one likes a complainer?" Isn't it the task of the cultural critic to tell us something we didn't already know what cultural forms mean, instead of lecturing us about our manners?

Even aside from its limpness as cultural analysis, Hughes's unwillingness to treat the complaints of the citizenry with any seriousness lends *Culture of Complaint* a complete lack of political coherence. Although fancying himself something of a populist politically, speaking favorably of "history from below" and empathizing with the fact that elected government doesn't represent the needs of the middle class, Hughes can't quite grasp that the middle classes, whose political aspirations he speaks so knowingly of, are precisely the audiences of all the culture he so despises: TV, and his special bête noir, these daytime talk shows. He hates talk-show guests because they complain too much—about their childhood sexual abuse, for example. Complaints should be confined to the sphere of electoral politics under the Hughes plan; complaints articulated within the sphere of culture enrage him. They're in bad taste. The idea that anyone might have legitimate grounds for complaint doesn't seem to register—apparently the woman raped by her father should just buck up. He hates the confessional mode and the autobiographical moment, and in his zeal to enforce tenuous oppositions between high and low culture, Hughes, *Time* magazine's art critic, overlooks the fact that the autobiographical has been one of those leitmotifs of culture since the first handprint on the cave wall. Given his dedication to propping up increasingly nominal distinctions—not only between high and low culture, but between the cultural and the political—Hughes can't fathom the possibility that the explosion of talk-show complaint might have something to do with his own point that there's no articulation of middle-class needs and aspirations in traditional electoral politics. For Hughes, a vote for Ross Perot is a matter for interpretation, but going on a daytime talk show is simply vulgar, because this cultural critic can't be bothered to imagine an answer to the question of why anyone watches TV. Why do more people watch daytime TV than vote? Presumably because there's some meaning being created there: for audiences these *are* spheres of complexity, of gratification, identification, and aspiration.

Hindered by the critical assumption that "low" forms of culture are devoid of meaning or seriousness, critics of the Hughes persuasion are able to overlook the obvious fact that hovering not too far beneath the surface of these ignoble genres—whether talk shows or pornography—are the same sorts of conundrums and questions that have plagued political theorists and philosophers for millennia. If you can view daytime TV minus the routine snobbish condescension, it's fairly apparent that animating and interwoven through the marital sniping and family hatred are serious questions: What is the nature of love?

How do you act ethically when your desires are in conflict with someone else's? Is human nature fundamentally selfish or benevolent? What is the personal price of cultural conformity, versus the social violence exacted on nonconformity? What does it mean to be human in the late twentieth century? These questions, although debated in ordinary language and in the idiom of experience (as opposed to abstraction or an academic vocabulary), probably occur in these contexts because philosophy is now an academic profession conducted in abstruse language, and official political discourse consists of vacant platitudes and blatant lies, and neither are places where ordinary concerns or issues of satisfaction, pleasure, or fulfillment can be articulated. None of this is to say that daytime talk shows are consistently intelligent, progressive, or always come up with the right answers, but then of course neither do any other forms of political or philosophical discourse.

It's hard to trust a social critic who claims to respect the political aspirations of the middle classes while sneering so contemptuously at their forms of cultural expression. From Robert Hughes to Allan Bloom (whose equally dictatorial cultural pronouncements are discussed in chapter 5), what we're offered in the name of cultural criticism lately, are arbitrary assertions and "standards" meant to raise the popular classes out of unworthiness and vulgarity. But this contempt for popular culture is a thinly disguised contempt for its audiences. The disdain of intellectuals for the masses has a long history, of course, as does the utilization of culture as a site for moral instruction and uplift.[17] But this is a form of political contempt as well, which means that it's time that the book-buying public stops lapping up the top-down guilt trips of these pointy-headed intellectuals, whose mission is to transform culture into a place for the dissemination of authority and the reinstallation of social controls.

***

Fat pornography takes its audiences on another ride altogether. Affirming and celebrating the fat body against a universal chorus of fat loathing, it's a safe haven for the defiance of social norms and proprieties, and for the fat body's complaints against all the significations of thinness. Fat pornography aligns itself against the thin body's chicken-hearted aspirations for order and control and opposes its conformist desire to simply take up an assigned place in the regime of the normal.

In fat pornography, no one is dieting. These bodies aren't undergoing transformation. Cascading mounds of flab, mattress-size buttocks, breasts like sagging, overfilled water balloons, meaty, puckered, elephantine thighs, and forty- to fifty-inch waistlines are greeted with avid sexual enthusiasm. The more cellulite the better. Magazines like *Plumpers and Big Women* encourage R-E-S-P-E-C-T toward their models and fat women everywhere; the feature stories and bios detailing the likes and dislikes of a 350-pound pinup are written with the same breathless awe of an *Esquire* feature on Cindy Crawford. Fat pornography has its own stars, and its canon of video classics with the requisite spinoffs and sequels. Teighlor, one of the biggest stars (in all senses of the word), even has her own fantasy love doll.

Gay male fat porn is focused less on soft fat than on bulk: bodies in the 250- to 300-pound range or, to use the vernacular, the "teddy bear." Teddy bears are beefy, barrel-chested, pot-bellied, and most important, hairy: *Bulk Male* is like a full-body Hair Club for Men ad or a shower drain's worst nightmare—carpets of chest hair, back hair, full beards. Here the operative turn-on terms are "husky," "bearlike," and "grizzly," although articles also swoon over big-bellied TV icons like John Goodman, Ed Asner, Carroll O'Connor, and Hoss Cartwright. "Daddy bear" Charles Kuralt is held in particular esteem.

Fat porn's mission is to bring fat out of the closet and deliver it up for public viewing. Here you have the unhindered flaunting of fat, and the assertion of the fat body's sexual existence. Where else can you find stretch marks, cellulite, weight-gain, and flabby thighs publicly represented? Displaying fat at all is socially objectionable; to be fat in public is to be a problem, a subject for endless commentary and jokes—consider Roseanne, Liz Taylor, Oprah, all of whose bodies have been sites for very public melo-dramas of transformation. Ridiculed when fat, heaped with exag-gerated acclaim and tributes when thin: the culture seems to have an insatiable interest in these transformations. When Oprah loses weight, even the *New York Times* reports it.

Some fat porn—both gay and straight, both videos and magazines—falls into the category of hard-core, meaning that penetration takes place. Given that hard-core is structured around a specific conclusion, that is, the act of penetration (gen-erally with certain specified detours along the way, namely oral sex), its narrative structure has a certain inevitability, a sense of purpose and direction. But even within hard-core there are formal variations: for example, whether the act of penetration is treated as a "scene" or as a "narrative." That is, whether the act is simply portrayed, or whether it's described as having a tem-poral dimension that unfolds and develops. The distinction between the "scene" and the "narrative" is one of the ongoing debates in theories about how memories are encoded, one debate being whether different types of memories—say, trau-matic memories—are encoded differently, perhaps as "flash-backs" or scenes. It's curious that pornography, a form of fantasy suspended somewhere between the dream, the wish, and the memory (and perhaps even invoking traumatic memory, i.e., the "primal scene"), should rely on the same aesthetic devices and perambulate the same aesthetic ground.[18]

A hard-core video like *Life in the Fat Lane* simply presents a series of scenes of quite gigantic women having sex with vari-ous normal-sized men. (There is a structuring device here: a tuxedoed master of ceremonies introduces each segment and then, of course, has his own moment in the sun at the end.) *Bulk Male*, a magazine, is similarly nonnarrative, simply offering up stills of hefty, hirsute men engaged in lumbering sex acts. But a magazine like *Jumbo Jezebel* is organized narratively, recounting, through a series of quite artful color stills, the courtship of a cheerful, curly-haired fat woman. We open with Jezebel, dressed to the nines in a ruffled print frock, black lace stockings, bejeweled, made up, and awaiting her gentleman suitor. He arrives, and the story moves from a kiss on the hand, to tentative fondling, to open-mouthed kisses . . . and as the evening progresses, from heavy petting to oral sex, penetration, and the inevitable cum shot. All of this takes place in a quite beautiful antique- and art-filled room, with most of the action occurring on a lush black leather couch; between the decor, which says "parvenu," and the bodies, which say "wrong side of the tracks," all sorts of narrative potential beyond the penetration plot gets put into circulation.

But other examples of the genre exist simply to display vistas of fat without any pretext such as penetration. Since their only structuring principle *is* fat, these videos take on something of the formless, meandering quality of absurdist theater. In *Mother Load I*, two very, very fat women in stretchy lingerie (with a combined weight of 790 pounds, the video's jacket copy helpfully informs us) spend an hour discussing whether or not they should go shopping. Asks one fat roommate confrontationally, "Should we go shopping?" "We don't need anything," replies the other. "I want to go shopping," says the first, plangently. This is a film with the timeless circularity of *Waiting for Godot*—you just know they're never going to get to go shopping. Instead, they don bright red boxing gloves (making a visually striking tableau against the bright blue walls of the bedroom) and begin boxing each other as a way to work out these minor domestic differences. They batter away while the camera roves around, over and between mountains of soft, quivering blubber in extremely long, unedited takes (clearly a *nouvelle vague* influence at work here) as the two "roommates" get progressively more out of breath. Finally they collapse on the bed and do some perfunctory fondling of each other. Eventually some of the lingerie comes off, and the frame fills with rolls and rolls of fat, and the camera gets as close as it can without causing injury—it seems to want to lodge itself between those deep pleats of flesh and take up residence as these two huge bodies heave and crash together like some ancient race of flabby female Titans. Like theater of the absurd for the consumer age, it ends where it started: "We forgot to go shopping." "I almost forgot. I want to go shopping." Other than fat and its sustenance, the human situation seems quite devoid of purpose or meaning here; but still, we don our boxing gloves and go on.

Dimensions is a magazine put out by and for "fat admirers," men who are sexually attracted to fat women and feel themselves to be part of a beleaguered, oppressed, and ridiculed minority for this alarming preference—which these days has certainly supplanted homosexuality as "the love that dare not speak its name." We'll refer to these men (as they themselves do) as "FAs." *Dimensions* is available only in hard-core porn stores despite its subdued content (no nudity), which consists of photo spreads of quite fat lingeried models, along with articles and self-help columns about getting along as an FA in a culture that places this kind of preference somewhere on a spectrum between farcical and criminally perverse. Articles concern themselves with the social difficulties and psychological complexities of dating fat women, whose self-esteem is often negligible and self-hatred high. What happens when you introduce your fat wife to your unsuspecting colleagues, or when your fat girlfriend goes on a diet? How do you deal with stares or, worse, rude comments on the street? And there are articles by fat women, for whom FAs are sometimes a mixed blessing, many of them Don Juans, say the articles, for whom fat women are interchangeable. Or they're looking for their mothers, or are untrustworthy, or ambivalent, or just generally dogs. Really, it sounds pretty much like your standard single heterosexual woman's complaint list about men, which is sort of the point. Maybe fat admirers aren't so very different from thin admirers, except for the small issue of the culture's scorn at their willful defiance of "normal" fetishes and sexual preferences.

Dimensions grew out of what's known as the "size acceptance movement" and takes an activist position in relation to the indignities and physical dangers inflicted on the fat, which range from run-of-the-mill discrimination to stereotypical media portrayals to controversial and highly risky weight loss surgeries (which is, according to *Dimensions*, a billion-dollar-a-year medical industry with an alarmingly high fatality rate). On the other hand, its articles can display an irritating tendency to whininess, frequently, for example, reproaching fat women themselves for the travails and oppressed minority status of male FAs, given that fat women can be just as uncomfortable with a man admiring their bodies as is the larger fat-hating society. There's a lively dialogue carried out between one faction, generally represented by fat women, whose optimistic position is that weight and size shouldn't be an acceptable criterion for judging worth ("love me for myself"), and a second faction, men who are positively turned on by fat women and have a strong preference for fat women. Some even have erotic weight *gain* fantasies about women (a group known to insiders as "feeders"). This subculture within the subculture struggles for acceptance of what is to many, even in this community, an unacceptable fantasy, with some women taking the feminist position that the weight gain fantasy is another form of male control, merely the flip side of those men in the general culture who insist their partners lose weight, since both versions employ the same tactics of cajolery, coercion, bribery, and domination about food and poundage.

This debate will likely seem bizarre to the noninitiate, particularly if you neglect to consider how intensely issues of size so routinely enter into even mainstream dating and mating rituals. Personal ads, for example, whatever the publication in which they appear, are typically rigorous in their specifications about bodily preferences: "slim," "weight proportional to height," "no chubbies" are common requests for both gays and straights. And these sorts of criteria obviously apply to every form of mate selection for quite a lot of the "nonperverse" population. To have a rigid sexual preference for a "slim" partner, even over, say, a fat Nobel Prize laureate, is a culturally acceptable and far from surprising sexual aim. But then issues of size, in general, are a recurring motif in sexual attraction, from the routine issue of height preferences for both men and women, to male attention to female breast size, to women's emerging (although sometimes ironic and retaliatory) attention to penis size. Of course, size is a pivotal, recurring motif in the culture generally. An interest in issues of scale, particularly the gigantic, occupies much cultural attention across a range of sites, from children's literature to sports "giants" (and the tacit acceptance of steroids to produce them), to cultural icons like Arnold Schwarzenegger, whose acting talents alone were perhaps not what propelled him so firmly into the cultural imagination. The gigantic has always been the subject of mythology. With the invention of officialdom and its institutions—church and state—the gigantic is appropriated from mythology for pragmatic ends: vastness, grandeur, and the massive scale of monuments and official architecture became ways of symbolizing the power of institutions and the insignificance of individuals; the hugeness of early cathedrals, for example, dwarfing the human with their immensity, were calculated to attract worshipful converts.[19]

Largeness seems to invite cultural ambivalence. Note also that largeness comes packaged in two gendered varieties. When soft and fat, it connotes the maternal and aggravates our tangled imaginative relation to issues of consumption—and by extension, issues of resources, distribution, and equity. When vast and hard—the gigantic—it connotes patriarchal masculinity: a way of symbolizing power and its abuses. Perhaps the systematic way the fat are stripped of social power symbolically stages the overthrow of sovereignty that symbolizes its authority through scale, both maternal and paternal. Unfortunately for those large humans who bear the ignominy of our hostile and threatened fascination with them.

The culture's anxiety about fat is endless, as is its hypocrisy. And it's safe to say that any issue of physical appearance impacts disproportionately on women. Everywhere in pop culture one finds thoughtful, concerned reports on the social plagues of anorexia and bulimia side by side with diet tips and fashion photos of waif models. But liking fat in current American culture makes you a "fetishist" whose sexuality is, by definition, "pornographic." Perhaps this indicates just how thoroughly pornography and fetishism are shifting social categories whose relation to the larger culture is one of defiance, transgression, and even social critique.

Pornography's celebration of fat, even its "objectification" of fat women, is in defiance of all societal norms and social controls. (And as on the "Fat Greeting Cards" show, these questions of exploitation don't seem to get raised about fat men models: no one seems too concerned about whether all those bearded male teddy bears are being exploited or ridiculed, or are causing other fat men to suffer.) Pornography's insistence on visibility for fat forces the spectacle of fat *as* fat, rather than as an array of connotations. Fat is what our culture, for all of the reasons suggested, doesn't want to look at. Pornography, in response, puts it on view. Fat pornography commemorates bodies that defy social norms, it solicits an erotic identification with bodies that are unresponsive to social control—with voracious, demanding, improper, non–upwardly mobile, socially transgressive bodies. What this and other pornography provides, in the aesthetic realm, is a free zone to defy the dictates and the homogeneity imposed on aesthetics, on sexuality, and on bodies. For those who aren't fat admirers, the disbelief and incredulity (and I suspect it's quite visceral in many cases) in the notion that enormously fat bodies can be in any nonperverse way beautiful, even a turn-on, shows just how deeply these social dictates are embedded in our psyches, how they construct our very mode of seeing the world. Pornography causes distress to those sensibilities, which have been so cannily shaped by our culture to appear, so falsely, as "natural." It also—as does *Hustler*—never lets us forget just how firmly class based those sensibilities are, and how devoted to shoring up class distinctions. For all of these reasons, instead of seeking to suppress the pornographic, we might instead regard it as performing a social service: one of revealing these cultural sore spots, of elucidating not only the connection between sex and the social, but between our desires, our "selves," and the casual everyday brutality of cultural conformity.

Four

Disgust and Desire:
Hustler Magazine

When *Hustler* publisher Larry Flynt was shot outside a Georgia courtroom in 1978 in an assassination attempt that left him paralyzed from the waist down, the nation hardly mourned. News reports of the shooting took an ironic tone (*Time* billed it "The Bloody Fall of a Hustler"). There were no candlelight vigils outside his hospital room or impassioned calls for the nation's prayers, even though when a similar fate befell Alabama governor George Wallace six years earlier, Wallace was instantly converted from southern racist to elder statesman in the national consciousness (and actually went on to win substantial support from black voters in his 1982 gubernatorial race after renouncing his segregationist ways). An avowed white supremacist named Joseph Paul Franklin was indicted for the Flynt shooting, but never tried.[1]

Flynt's spinal nerves were severed, leaving him both paralyzed and in constant pain. He became a paranoid recluse, barricading himself behind the steel door to the bedroom of his Bel

Air mansion, surrounded by thuggish bodyguards. Wife Althea
Leasure, then twenty-seven and a former go-go dancer, took control of the multi-million-dollar Flynt empire, comparing herself
to a rogue version of *Washington Post* publisher Katharine
Graham, a woman whose publishing career also followed her
husband's demise. Although Flynt is now a wheelchair-bound
paraplegic, it seems impossible to muster sympathy for his plight.
He'd made a national nuisance of himself, like some attention-
grabbing overgrown adolescent boy mooning the guests at a
church social, and the attitude of the nation appeared to be that
he pretty much got what he deserved.

Maybe the roadblock to a Wallace-like sentimental reha-
bilitation of Flynt was that his career as a pornographer spilled
out into the political arena rather than being confined to the
pages of his smut sheet (and the only thing he renounced was
his weird, highly publicized preshooting conversion to Christianity). Flynt had fashioned himself into a one-man bug up the
nation's ass, single-mindedly dedicating himself to his self-
appointed role as loudmouthed whistle-blower on what he regarded as our national hypocrisy. His favored tactic was to
systematically and extravagantly violate, in the most profoundly
offensive way possible, each and every deeply held social taboo,
norm, and propriety he could identify. The nation responded
with its kneejerk response to any perceived insult or injury: the
lawsuit.

As with transvestite porn and fat porn, pornography can
provide a home for those narratives exiled from sanctioned
speech and mainstream political discourse, making pornography, in essence, an oppositional political form. If this seems to
attribute too much credit or too much intelligence to mere smut,
recall that most recently it has, in fact, been pornography—via
Larry Flynt—that has had a decisive effect on expanding the
perimeters of political speech in this country. *Not* the main-

stream press, the political left, or the avant-garde. The 1988 Rehnquist Supreme Court decision against Moral Majoritarian Jerry Falwell's $45-million suit against Flynt and *Hustler* (for a mercilessly pornographic antireligious parody) was the biggest victory for freedom of the press in years; its sweeping protection of pornographic political satire also, perhaps unwittingly, reconfirmed pornography's historic role *as* political speech.

Since the democratizing invention of print and the birth of a print culture, pornography has been a favored strategy of social criticism, slinging muddy handfuls of obscenity and blasphemy at the power of political and religious authorities. Who responded, of course, by doing everything possible to eliminate it. *Hustler*'s fusion of nudity and vulgarity with attacks on established political power, organized religion, and class privilege places it squarely within this five-century-long rabble-rousing tradition. Its commitment to disobedience and insubordination, to truth-telling—as it sees truth, anyway—and exposing social hypocrisy, prompts the question of whether it's *Hustler*'s *political* project (fueled by Flynt's long-standing grudge match with the state) that makes it the most reviled instance of mass-circulation porn. In other words, maybe it's not just those naked women. Historically, pornography was defined as what the state was determined to suppress.[2] *Hustler*'s entire publishing history, in line with tradition, has also been punctuated by extraordinarily numerous attempts at regulation and suppression, both public and private.

Larry Flynt was born in Appalachia, in Magoffin County, Kentucky (then the poorest county in America), the son of a pipe welder, making him very much a product of the white trash demographic his magazine appears to address. He quit school after the eighth grade, joined the navy at fourteen with a forged birth certificate, got out, worked in a General Motors auto assembly plant, and foresightedly parlayed $1,500 in savings into a chain of go-go bars in Ohio called the Hustler Clubs. The magazine originated as a two-page newsletter for the bars, and the rest was rags to riches: Flynt's income was as high as $30 million a year when *Hustler* was at its peak circulation of over 2 million. At this point he built himself a scale replica of the cabin he grew up in down in the basement of his mansion. Its purpose: to remind him of his roots. The model is said to be replete with chickenwire, hay, and a three-foot lifelike statue of the chicken he claims to have lost his virginity to at age eight. Who says he's an unsentimental guy? (When Flynt started his magazine *Chic,* having little facility with a French accent, he insisted his staff pronounce it "Chick"—another homage, maybe.[3])

Since *Hustler*'s inception, Flynt has probably been hauled through the civil and criminal courtrooms of the nation more often than anyone in recent memory, on an astonishing array of obscenity, libel, and criminal charges. (These in turn spawned assorted contempt charges—fines and jail time—given his propensity for indecorous courtroom behavior.) In no particular order: Flynt was sued by rival *Penthouse* publisher Bob Guccione for invasion of privacy over a number of venomous cartoons chronicling his sexual exploits (and in a separate suit, by a female *Penthouse* executive who thought *Hustler* had libeled her by printing that she'd contracted VD from Guccione). He was sued by socialite-novelist Jackie Collins, after the magazine published nude photos it incorrectly identified as the nude authoress (she wound up having to pay court costs after an initial $40-million verdict in her favor was thrown out on appeal). Antipornography feminist Andrea Dworkin brought a $150-million lawsuit for invasion of her privacy, which was thrown out by the Supreme

125

Court; her lawyer, the not particularly publicity-shy Gerry Spence, then filed suit when *Hustler* named him its "Asshole of the Month" for representing Dworkin.

Flynt was fined $10,000 a day—upped to $20,000 a day— when he refused to turn over to the feds tapes he claimed he possessed documenting a government frame of the dashing and bankrupt automaker John DeLorean on drug charges. Flynt, who didn't actually know DeLorean, but had apparently formed an imaginative identification with him as a victim of the same "repressive establishment," managed to place himself at the center of the high-profile DeLorean trial by presenting CBS News with audiotapes of mysterious origin revealing a key FBI informant threatening DeLorean's daughter when DeLorean tried to back out of the drug frame. No charges were brought against columnist Jack Anderson, who also claimed to have copies of the tapes (and also refused to divulge their source). Flynt, however, not commanding the journalistic legitimacy of a Jack Anderson in the eyes of the court, served over six months in a federal penitentiary on contempt charges, which were eventually dismissed.

Following the assassination attempt, which took place outside yet another courtroom where he was being tried, again, for obscenity, Flynt's public behavior became increasingly bizarre. (In constant pain, he'd become addicted to morphine and Dilaudid, finally detoxing to methadone.) He appeared in court sporting an American flag as a diaper and was arrested. At a 1984 Los Angeles trial, described by the *L.A. Times* as "legal surrealism," his own attorney requested permission to gag his unruly client; after an "obscene outburst," Flynt, like Black Panther and Chicago Seven coconspirator Bobby Seale before him, was bound and gagged at his own trial.[4]

The same year the FCC was compelled to issue an opinion on Flynt's threat to force television stations to show his X-rated presidential campaign commercials. In a new bid for the nation's love and attention, he was running for president, as a Republican, with Native American activist Russell Means as his vice-presidential candidate. Or because, as he eloquently put it, "I am wealthy, white, pornographic, and, like the nuclear-mad cowboy Ronnie Reagan, I have been shot for what I believe in." Flynt's new compulsion was to find loopholes in the nation's obscenity laws, and with typical monomania he vowed to use his presidential campaign to test those laws by insisting TV stations show campaign commercials featuring hard-core sex acts. (The equal time provision of Federal Communications Act prohibits censorship of any ad in which a candidate's voice or picture appears.[5])

Then there was his stormy, anxiety-ridden love affair with the First Amendment, with Flynt, like one half of some inseparable codependent couple, forever testing, demanding, entreating its fidelity. Would it betray him, or bestow its favors once more? In 1986, a federal judge ruled that the U.S. Postal Service couldn't constitutionally prohibit Flynt from sending copies of *Hustler* to members of Congress, a ruling stemming from Flynt's beneficent decision to confer free copies upon elected officials so they could be "well informed on all social issues and trends." (More than 260 complained, ungraciously, to the postal service.)

But Flynt's most renowned First Amendment contretemps was the $45-million federal libel suit brought by an unamused Jerry Falwell over the notorious Campari "first time" ad parody, which suggested that Falwell's "first time" had occurred with his mother behind an outhouse. Flynt turned up in court ensconced in a gold-plated wheelchair; a Virginia jury dismissed the libel charge but awarded Falwell $200,000 for intentional infliction of emotional distress. A federal district court upheld the verdict, but when it landed in the Rehnquist Supreme Court the judgment was reversed by a unanimous Rehnquist-written decision that the Falwell parody was not reasonably believable, and thus fell into the category of satire, an art form often "slashing and one-sided."

This Supreme Court decision significantly extended the freedom of the press won in the 1964 *New York Times v. Sullivan* decision, which ruled that libel could be found in cases of "reckless disregard." For the press, this was one of the most significant legal triumphs in recent years, and they unanimously hailed the decision as "an endorsement of robust political debate," which promised to end the influx of what they regarded as "pseudo-libel suits" brought by money-grubbing celebrities with hurt feelings. A grateful national press grappled with the contradiction between its relief at the outcome and its profound desire to distance itself from Flynt and *Hustler,* generally concluding that the existence of excrescences like *Hustler* is the price of freedom of the press, with frequent recourse to platitudes about "strange bedfellows." As political cartoonist Pat Oliphant put it, with morning-after pensiveness, "You're forced into bed with very strange people when you believe in the right of free expression . . . we all had to go to bat for Larry Flynt—not that we wanted to, and you felt like taking a shower afterward."

In the last analysis, however squeamish those who value the First Amendment are about that one-night stand with *Hustler,* it's been Larry Flynt's apparently compulsive need to pit himself against the state's enforcement of bodily proprieties, and against its desire to regulate how sex and the body can be represented, that betrays to what extent these *are* political issues. Otherwise, why the state's compelling interest in the matter?

For Flynt, and within the pages of *Hustler,* sex has always been a political, not a private, matter. The *Hustler* body is a battleground of opposing social and cultural forces: religious morality, class pretensions, and feminist censoriousness duke it out with the armies of bodily vulgarity, kinky fantasy, and unromanticized fucking. Although often lumped together in the popular imagination into an unholy trinity with *Penthouse* and *Playboy,* the other two top-circulation men's magazines, *Hustler* is actually quite a different beast in any number of respects, setting itself apart, from its inception, with its antiestablishment, anarchist-libertarian politics. But it also outstripped the other two in its unprecedented explicitness and raunch (unprecedented for a mass-circulation, as opposed to hard-core, magazine), and through its crusade *for* explicitness, shrilly accusing the other two of not really delivering the goods. The strategy paid off: *Hustler* captured a third of the men's market with its entrée into the field in 1974 by being the first of the torrid trio to reveal pubic hair. *Penthouse* swiftly followed suit, in response to which a *Hustler* pictorial presented its model shaved; *Hustler* then further upped the explicitness ante and created a publishing scandal by displaying a glimpse of pubic hair on its cover in July 1976. This was *Hustler*'s unique commemoration of our nation's bicentennial: the model wore stars and stripes, although far too few of them.

Throughout these early years *Hustler*'s pictorials persisted in showing more and more of what had previously been the forbidden zone (the "pink" in *Hustler*-speak), with *Penthouse* struggling to keep up and *Playboy,* whose focus had always been above the waist anyway, keeping a discreet distance. In *Hustler*'s ideology, *Playboy* and *Penthouse*'s relative discretion about the female body makes them collaborationists with the forces of repression and social hypocrisy that *Hustler* had set itself the task of exposing. It continually railed against their lack of explicitness, their coyness and veiling of the body—by *Hustler*'s standards—which smacks of all the forms of social hypocrisy that depend on decorum and civility, on not naming names or saying it the way it really is, on docility in the face of secret abuses of power and privilege. The veiled "private" body is analogous to the hidden government (the Iran-Contra scandal was a shining moment for *Hustler*), analogous to the hidden sources of wealth of the ruling classes, which secretly the rest of us are paying for through our labor, and to the hidden abuses of power and privilege that make the social engine chug so smoothly along, benefiting the few, but not the *Hustler* reader.

Not for *Hustler* are the upwardly mobile professional-class fantasies that fuel the *Playboy* and *Penthouse* imaginations, or the celebrity interviews that cozy up to the power elite and rich media big shots. *Hustler* addresses itself to what it describes as a working-class audience, ranting madly against all forms of power—whether state sanctioned or criminally insane—by making them indistinguishable from one another. ("*Hustler* has taken readers into the twisted minds of Hillside Strangler Kenneth Bianchi, the Republican National Committee and Los Angeles' hitmen cops" as it put it in a typical piece of self-promotion.) The catalog of social resentments *Hustler* trumpets, particularly against class privilege, makes it by far the most openly class-antagonistic mass-circulation periodical of any genre. (And after all, class privilege is the dirty little secret of all national and electoral politics: face it, no welfare moms, homeless, unemployed, no blue-collar workers represent the nation in those hallowed legislative halls of our "representative" democracy.)

Hustler was, from the beginning, determined to violate all the taboos observed by its more classy men's-rag brethren. It began by introducing penises. This was a sight so verboten in traditional men's magazines that its strict prohibition impels you to wonder about just what traumas the sight of a penis might provoke in the male viewer. (And of course, the focus on "female objectification" in critiques of hard-core pornography also symptomatically ignores the truth of heterosexual hard-core, which is that, by definition, it features both women *and* men, which allows men *and* women to view male *and* female bodies in sexual contexts.)

From its inception, *Hustler* made it its mission to disturb and unsettle its readers, both psychosexually and sociosexually, by interrogating the typical men's magazine conventions of sexuality. *Hustler*'s early pictorials included pregnant women, middle-aged women (horrified news commentaries referred to "geriatric pictorials"), hugely fat women, hermaphrodites, amputees, and in a moment of true *frisson* for your typical heterosexual male, a photo spread of a preoperative transsexual, doubly well-endowed. *Hustler* continued to provoke reader outrage with a 1975 interracial pictorial (black male, white female), which according to *Hustler* was protested by both the KKK and the NAACP. It enraged readers with explicit photo spreads of the consequences of venereal disease, graphic war carnage, and other in-your-face pictorials. You looked to *Hustler* for what you wouldn't get the chance to see elsewhere, for the kind of visual materials the rest of society devotes itself to not portraying and not thinking about. (And *Hustler*'s influence on the genre has been such that by 1991, *Playboy* was willing to scandalize its somewhat less adventuresome readers by running a photo spread of a beautiful *post*operative transsexual, unintentionally reminding readers that the requirement to become a *Playboy* centerfold is, as usual, simply vast amounts of cosmetic surgery and silicone, whether you're born male *or* female.)

Even beyond its explicitness, *Hustler*'s difference from *Playboy* and *Penthouse* is in the sort of female body it imagines. The *Hustler* body is an unromanticized body: no Vaselined lenses or soft focus here. This is neither the airbrushed top-heavy fantasy body of *Playboy*, nor the slightly cheesy, ersatz opulence of *Penthouse*, whose lingeried and sensitive crotch shots manage to transform female genitalia into ersatz *objets d'art*. The sexuality *Hustler* delivers is far from normative, with the most polymorphous array of sexual preferences regarded as equivalent to "normal sex," whether they adhere to the standard heterosexual teleology of penetration or not. Male-male sexuality is even raised as a possibility. And in stark distinction to the *Playboy/Penthouse* body, the *Hustler* body has an interior, not just a suntanned surface. It's insistently material, defiantly vulgar, corporeal. In fact, the *Hustler* body is often a gaseous, fluid-emitting, *embarrassing* body, one continually defying the strictures of social manners and mores and instead governed by its lower intestinal tract: a body threatening to erupt at any moment. *Hustler's* favorite joke is someone accidentally defecating in church.

Particularly in its cartoons, but also in its editorials and political humor, *Hustler* devotes itself to what we might call "grossness": an obsessive focus on the lower half of the body, and on the processes (and products) of elimination. Its joke techniques are based on exaggeration and inversion, which have long been staples of pornographic political satire. In fact, the *Hustler* worldview is quite similar to that of Rabelais, the sixteenth-century French social satirist, whose emphasis was also on the bodily and the grotesque.[6] And although Rabelais has now taken up his place in the canon of classics, he was, in his own day, forced to flee France when his work was condemned for heresy (and placed on the *Index of Forbidden Books* by the Council of Trent) in something of a prequel to Larry Flynt's run-ins with current obscenity law.

Hustler's quite Rabelaisian exaggeration of everything improper is apparent in even a partial inventory of the subjects it finds fascinating. Fat women, assholes, monstrous and gigantic sexual organs, body odors (the notorious scratch-and-sniff centerfold, which due to "the limits of the technology," Flynt apologized, strongly reeked of lilacs), anal sex, and anything that exudes from the body: piss, shit, semen, menstrual blood, particularly when they sully public, sanitary, or sanctified sites. And especially farts: farting in public, farting loudly, Barbara Bush farting, priests and nuns farting, politicians farting, the professional classes farting, the rich farting. All of this is certainly a far remove from the sleek, laminated *Playboy/Penthouse* body. As *Newsweek* once complained of *Hustler*, "The contents of an average issue read like something Krafft-Ebing might have whispered to the Marquis de Sade. . . . *Hustler* is into erotic fantasies involving excrement, dismemberment, and the sexual longings of rodents . . . where other skin slicks are merely kinky, *Hustler* can be downright frightful. . . . The net effect is to transform the erotic into the emetic."[7]

It's not clear if what sets *Newsweek* to crabbing is that *Hustler* transgresses proper social mores or that *Hustler* violates men's magazine conventions of sexuality. On both fronts it's transgressive. In fact, on *every* front *Hustler* devotes itself to producing generalized Rabelaisian transgression. According to Larry Flynt in a reflective moment, "Tastelessness is a necessary tool in challenging preconceived notions in an uptight world where people are afraid to discuss their attitudes, prejudices and misconceptions." This too is not so far from Rabelais, who also used the lower body as a symbolic attack on the pompous false seriousness of high culture, church, and state.[8]

Hustler's insistent, repetitious return to the imagery of the body out of control, rampantly transgressing social norms and sullying property and proprieties, can't fail to raise certain political questions. Anthropologists have observed that the human body is universally employed as a symbol for human society, and that control over the body is always a symbolic expression of

social control.[9] The body and the social are both split into higher
and lower strata, with images or symbols of the upper half of
the body making symbolic reference to society's upper echelons
—the socially powerful—while the lower half of the body and
its symbols (*Hustler*'s métier) makes reference to the lower
tiers—those without social power. Given this reading, the meaning of the symbolic inversion *Hustler* performs—in which the
lower stratum dominates and indeed triumphs over the forces
of reason, power, and privilege—starts to have some political
resonance.[10]

Symbolically deploying the improper body as a mode of
social sedition also follows logically from the fact that the body
is the very thing those forms of power under attack—government, religion, bourgeois manners and mores—devote themselves to keeping "in its place." Control over the body has long
been considered essential to producing an orderly work force, a
docile populace, a passive law-abiding citizenry. Just consider
how many actual laws are on the books regulating *how* bodies
may be seen and what parts may not, *what* you may do with your
body in public *and* in private, and it begins to make more sense
that the out-of-control, unmannerly body is precisely what
threatens the orderly operation of the status quo. Historically,
local carnivals were something of a release valve from the shack-
les of social control: seasonal or yearly festivals of improprieties,
where drunkenness, low humor, and grotesque, out-of-control
bodies rampaged and reigned.[11] As carnivals too became increasingly regulated and sanitized (and in our own day, expropriated
by big business: carnivals were certainly the predecessors of
today's sterile corporate-owned theme parks), other cultural expressions of the out-of-control body appear and are subject to
regulation. Like pornography. But the tethers of bodily propriety
have become so increasingly internalized, so much a cornerstone

of the modern self, that the grotesqueries of the sixteenth-century carnival would no doubt seem extraordinarily unnerving and unpleasurable to the contemporary citizen.

What we consider gross and disgusting is hardly some permanent facet of the human psyche: it's historically specific and relatively recent. According to social historian Norbert Elias, disgust only fully emerges in the course of the sixteenth century rise of individualism, during which time we see the invention of the concept of privacy as well: our various requirements about closed (and locked) bathroom doors, our own plates to eat from, and delicacy around sexual and bodily matters are all aspects of this same social process. Disgust is something precariously acquired in the course of the civilizing process (and a process that has to be recapitulated in the socialization of each individual modern child). During this social transformation, once communal activities—sleeping, sex, elimination, eating—became subject to new sets of rules of conduct and privatization. An increasingly heightened sense of disgust at the bodies and bodily functions of others emerged, and simultaneous with this process of privatization came a corresponding sense of shame about one's own body and its functions. Certain once-common behaviors become socially frowned on: spitting, scratching, farting, wiping your mouth on the tablecloth, or blowing your nose into your sleeve were replaced by increasingly detailed rules devoted to restraining the conduct of the body (and even how it might be spoken of) in public.

Historically speaking, manners have a complicated history as a mechanism of class distinction, that is, of separating the high from the low. Implements we now take for granted, like the fork and the handkerchief, were initially seen as upper-class affectations (you both blew your nose into and ate with your hands, and from communal dishes). Only gradually did they filter down through the social hierarchy. But as money rather than aristocratic origins became the basis for social distinctions, manners took on an increasing importance, and they too started disseminating down throughout the population. Although originally mechanisms of social distinction, these behavior reforms and increasingly refined manners were also progressively restructuring *internal* standards of privacy, disgust, shame, and embarrassment throughout the population, thus transforming both daily *and* inner life. As with any massive social transformation though, this was a gradual and incomplete process.

It was also a social transformation with the most profound consequences on individual psychology and subjectivity. As far more attention came to be paid to proprieties around elimination, to hygiene, to bodily odors, and to not offending others, thresholds of sensitivity and refinement in the individual psyche became correspondingly heightened. It wasn't just behavior being reformed, it was the entire structure of the psyche, with the most shameful and prohibited behaviors and impulses (those around sex and elimination) propelled into the realm of the unconscious. This split, which Freud would later describe with the terms "ego" and "id," is what would become the very substance of the modern individual. And the experience of disgust at what was once an ordinary part of daily life has become so completely part of our "nature" that defiance of bodily proprieties can result in actual physical revulsion. When we say of something disgusting "It made me sick," this can be a physical fact, revealing just how very deeply these codes have become embedded in who we are. And how threatening to our very *beings* transgressions of manners can be. (This is far from only an individual issue, as these codes of conduct became part of the implicit rationale of the imperial project as well: the lack of "civilization" of the inhabitants of other parts of the globe was always part of the justification for invading, colonizing, or enslaving them.[12])

Here's a clue about why *Newsweek* should get so crabby about *Hustler,* and why *Hustler,* with its anarchistic, antiestablishment, working-class politics, should seize on grossness as the perfect blunt instrument with which to register its protests. Here also is a way to think about why the state would be so interested in matters of the body and its symbols. The power of grossness is very simply its opposition to high culture and official culture, which feels the continual need to protect itself against the debasements of the low (the lower classes, low culture, the lower body . . .). When the social and the bodily are put side by side, it becomes apparent how grossness and erupting bodies manage to suggest the ongoing jeopardy (to those in power) and ongoing uncertainty of a social hierarchy only tenuously held in place through symbolic (and real) policing of the threats posed by rebellious bodies: by the unruly classes, by angry mobs. And apparently by at least some forms of pornography.

The history of disgust as a mechanism of class distinction is another reason the feminist antipornography movement is so politically problematic. There's a telling moment in the early antiporn documentary *Not a Love Story,* in which feminist author-poet (and former *Ms.* magazine editor) Robin Morgan turns up to register a genteel protest against pornography. Posed in her large book-lined living room, poet-husband Kenneth Pitchford (who appears to be wearing an ascot) at her side, she inveighs against a range of sexual practices: not only masturbation—on the grounds that it promotes political passivity—but also "superficial sex, kinky sex, appurtenances and [sex] toys" for, as she puts it "benumbing . . . normal human sensuality."

137

She then breaks into tears as she describes the experience of living in a society where pornographic media thrives.

Keep this scene in mind as you imagine the following, slightly less proper one, described in a letter to *Hustler* from "E.C.," a reader who introduces an account of an erotic experience involving a cruel-eyed, high-heeled dominatrix with this vivid self-description: "One night, trudging home from work— I gut chickens, put their guts in a plastic bag and stuff them back in the chicken's asshole—I varied my routine by stopping at a small pub. . . ."[13]

Let's allow these two scenes—one filmed, one literary— to stand in for the combative and mutually uncomprehending relation of *Hustler* and its critics. The stark differences in tone, setting, affect, and even accessories, usher in a generally off-limits topic: the relation between sexuality and class (or modes of representing them). In one corner we have a tearful Morgan, laboring for the filmmakers and their audience as a feminist intellectual, constructing, from a relatively privileged social position, a normative theory of sexuality that she endeavors to impose on the rest of the population. While "feminist intellectual" is not necessarily the highest-paying job category these days, it's quite a few steps up the social hierarchy from that of "E.C.," whose work is of a character that tends to be relegated to the lower rungs within a society (and a social division of labor) that categorizes jobs dealing with things that smell, or that for other reasons we prefer to hide from view—garbage, sewage, dirt, animal corpses—as of low status, both monetarily and socially.

E.C.'s letter, carefully (a lot more carefully than Morgan's pleas) framing his sexuality in relation to his material circumstances and with a keen awareness of how social distinctions operate in our culture, is typical of *Hustler* in its vulgarity, its explicitness about "kinky" sex, and in the insistent association between sexuality and class. *Hustler* consistently frames sex acts as occuring within historically and economically specific contexts, in distinction to the set of *universal* norms feminist Morgan attempts to disseminate downward. Morgan's vision of "normal human sensuality" neither comprehends nor includes E.C.'s night of bliss with his Mistress, who incidentally "mans" herself with just the kind of appurtenances Morgan seems to be referring to. (And can Morgan seriously mean to so blast "appurtenances" like the dildo, that distinguished emblem of feminist self-reliance?)

Hustler too offers its readers a "theory of sexuality," although unlike Morgan, *Hustler* isn't disseminating universal pronouncements. It offers an explicitly political analysis of power and the body, in addition to being explicit about its own class location. Comparing these two scenes—Morgan's living room versus E.C.'s night of kinky sex—it begins to appear that Morgan's tears, her sentiment, are performed *against* E.C.'s vulgarity, and that the desire to banish from one's existence the cause of one's distress has something of an historical imperative. Social distinctions are maintained through the expression of taste, disgust, and exclusion. Historically, the upper classes defined themselves against what they defined as dirty, low, repulsive, noisy, and contaminating: acts of exclusion that precisely maintained their identity as a class.[14] Disgust has a long and complicated history, central to which is the tendency of the emerging bourgeoisie to want to remove the distasteful from the sight of society (including, of course, dead animals, which might interest E.C., degutter of chickens), because as Norbert Elias puts it, "People in the course of the civilizing process seek to suppress in themselves every characteristic they feel to be animal."[15]

These gestures of disgust are crucial to the regulations surrounding the body, which has become so rigidly split into higher and lower stratum that tears—as Morgan so well demonstrates—become the only publicly permissible display of body fluids. The products of the body start to stack up into a set of neat oppositions: on the one side upper bodily productions, a heightened sense of delicacy, sentiment, refinement, and the social project of removing the distasteful from sight (and sight, of course, is at the top of the hierarchy of the senses central to Enlightenment identity and rationality); and on the other side, the lower body and *its* productions (shit, farts, semen— *Hustler*'s staple joke materials), the insistence on vulgarity and violations of the "proper" body. From this vantage point, Morgan's antipornography project, not to mention those tears—devoted as they are to concealing the unruly, unregulated body from view—can be seen as part of a centuries-long sociohistorical process, and one that plays an ongoing role in maintaining social hierarchies.

It's difficult to see feminist disgust in isolation and disgust at pornography as strictly a gender issue if you take into account the historic function of these sorts of gestures. Western feminism has often been accused of wearing blinders, of formulating itself strictly in relation to the experiences of white, upper-class women. Insofar as the feminist antiporn movement devotes itself to rehearsing the experience of disgust and attempting to regulate sexual imagery, the class issue will continue to be one of its formative blind spots. One might want to interpret feminist disgust as expressing *symbolically* the very real dangers that exist for women in the world. But the net effect is to displace those dangers onto a generalized disgust with sex and the body (or more specifically, onto heterosexual sex and the male body). Andrea Dworkin, for example, writes extensively about her disgust at semen, a lower bodily production which, she tells us, she regards as a form of "pollution."[16] Her disgust is her prerogative (as long as she doesn't attempt to enact legislation on the basis of it[17]), but even as mobilized against a perception of violation to the female body, it's more than problematic in a political movement devoted to achieving liberation and social equity.

As a feminist (not to mention a petit bourgeois and denizen of the academic classes), I too find myself often disgusted by *Hustler*. This is *Hustler* hitting its target, like some heat-seeking offense missile, because it's someone like me who's precisely *Hustler*'s ideal sitting duck. *Hustler* pits itself against not just the proper body, that holdover from the bourgeois revolution, but against all the current paraphernalia of yuppie professionalism. At its most obvious, *Hustler* is simply allergic to any form of social or intellectual affectation, squaring off like some maddened pit bull against the pretensions and the earning power of the professional classes: doctors, optometrists, dentists, and lawyers are favored targets. It's pissed off by liberals and particularly nasty to academics, who are invariably prissy and uptight. (An academic to his wife: "Eat your pussy? You forget, Gladys, I have a Ph.D.") It rants against the power of government, which is by definition corrupt, as are elected officials, the permanent government, even foreign governments. Of course it smears the rich against the wall, particularly rich women, and dedicates many, many pages to the hypocrisy of organized religion, with a nonstop parade of jokes on the sexual instincts of the clergy, the sexual possibilities of the crucifixion, the scam of the virgin birth, and the bodily functions of nuns, priests, and ministers.

These are just *Hustler*'s more manifest targets. Reading a bit deeper, its offenses create a detailed blueprint of the national cultural psyche. *Hustler*'s favored tactic is to zero in on a subject, an issue, an "unsaid" that the bourgeois imagination prefers to be unknowing about—those very problematic materials a protectively tight-assed culture has founded itself upon suppressing, and prohibits irreverent speech about. Things we would call "tasteless" at best, or might even become physically revulsed by: the physical detritus of aborted fetuses, how and where the homeless manage to relieve themselves (not much social attention devoted to this little problem), amputation, the proximity of sexual organs to those of elimination, the various uses to which liposuctioned fat might be put—any aspect of how the material body fares in our current society.[18]

A case in point, and one that subjected *Hustler* to national outrage: its two cartoons about former first lady Betty Ford's mastectomy. If we can distance ourselves from our automatic indignation for a moment, *Hustler* might be seen as posing, through the strategy of transgression, an interesting cultural question: Which subjects are taboo for even sick humor? It wasn't uncommon, following the *Challenger* explosion, to hear the sickest jokes about scattered body parts, while jokes about amputees and paraplegics are not unknown even on broadcast TV (and of course abound on the pages of *Hustler*); jokes about blindness are considered so benign that one involving blind bluesman Ray Charles was featured in a long-running "blind taste test" soda pop commercial. Yet mastectomy is one subject that appears to be completely off limits as a humorous topic. But back to amputees, perhaps a better comparison: apparently a man without a limb is considered less tragic by the culture at large, less mutilated, and less of a cultural problem than a woman without a breast. A mastectomy more of a tragedy than the deaths of the seven astronauts.

This offers some clues about the deep structure of a cultural psyche, as does our deeply felt outrage at *Hustler*'s transgression. After all, what *is* a woman without a breast in a culture that measures breasts as the measure of the woman? Not a fit subject for comment. It's a subject so veiled that it's not even available to the "working through" of the joke. (And a case once again, where *Hustler* seems to be deconstructing the codes of the typical men's magazine: where *Playboy* creates a fetish of the breast, and whose very *raison d'être* is the cultural obsession with them, *Hustler* perversely points out that materially speaking, they're merely tissue—another limb.)

One way to think about *Hustler*'s knack for locating and attacking the jugular of a culture's sensitivity is as intellectual work not unlike those classic anthropological studies that translate a culture into a set of structural oppositions (obsession with the breast/prohibition of mastectomy jokes), laying bare the structure of its taboos and arcane superstitions. (It's not only "primitive" cultures that have irrational taboos, after all.) In fact *Hustler* performs a similar cultural mapping to Mary Douglas's classic anthropological study *Purity and Danger*, which produces a comparable social blueprint. The vast majority of *Hustler* humor seems animated by the desire to violate what Douglas describes as "pollution" taboos and rituals. These are a society's set of beliefs, rituals, and practices having to do with dirt, order, and hygiene (and by extension, the pornographic), which vary from culture to culture. Douglas points out that such violations aren't entirely unpleasurable: confronting ambiguity, even revulsion and shock, isn't unrelated to the kinds of transgressions that make us laugh and give us pleasure in the realm of comedy and humor.[19]

That sense of pleasure and danger that violation of pollution taboos invokes in us clearly depends on the existence, within every culture, of symbolic maps or codes. These are, for the most part, only semiconscious. *Hustler*'s defilement isn't some isolated event: it can only engage our interest or provoke our anxiety or our disgust to the extent that our ideas about these things form a cultural system, and that this system matters enormously—to our society, and in our very beings. As Freud remarks in his study of humor, *Jokes and Their Relation to the Unconscious*, "Only jokes that have a purpose run the risk of meeting with people who do not want to listen to them." Given that so much of the *Hustler* idiom is couched in the joke form (as is much pornography), the pleasures and displeasures of jokes—jokes are often a coded way of saying something slightly transgressive—are probably not unrelated to the transgressive pleasures and displeasures of pornography.

Although Mary Douglas highlights the ambivalent pleasures of purity violations, confronting transgression and violation can be profoundly unpleasant, too, as *Hustler*'s many opponents so vehemently attest. For Freud, interestingly, this displeasure has mostly to do with gender and class. Freud first undertakes to categorize jokes according to their gender effects: for example, regarding excremental jokes (a staple of *Hustler* humor), Freud tells us that these jokes are targeted to both men and women, as we all experience a common sense of shame surrounding bodily functions. And it's true that *Hustler*'s numerous jokes on the proximity of the sexual organs to those of elimination, the confusion of assholes and vaginas, turds and penises, shit and sex (a typical example: a couple is fucking in a hospital room while someone in the next bed is getting an enema, all get covered with shit), aren't targeted to a particular gender. Unless, that is, we women put ourselves, more so than men, in the position of upholders of good taste.

But *obscene* humor, whose purpose is to verbally expose sexual facts and relations, is, for Freud, the result of male and female sexual discordancies, and the dirty joke is something like a seduction gone awry. The motive for (men's) dirty jokes is that women are incapable of tolerating undisguised sexuality, and this incapacity increases correspondingly as your educational and social level rise. Both men and women are subject to sexual inhibition or repression, but women, and especially upper-class women, are the most seriously afflicted in the Freudian world. So dirty jokes function as a sign for both sexual difference ("smut is like an exposure of the sexually different person to whom it is directed . . . it compels the person who is assailed to imagine the part of the body or the procedure in question") and class difference. If it weren't for women's lack of sexual willingness and uptight class refinement, the joke wouldn't be a joke, but a proposition: "If the woman's readiness emerges quickly the obscene speech has a short life; it yields at once to a sexual action," hypothesizes Freud hopefully.

This might all sound a bit Victorian, but it's also still true that pornographic images and jokes are aggressive to women because they're capable of causing discomfort. And they're capable of causing discomfort insofar as there are differing levels of sexual inhibition between at least some men and some women. And upper-classness or upper-class identification exacerbates this difference. (For Freud, even the form of the joke is classed, with a focus on joke "technique" associated with higher social classes and education levels, which explains something about how really stupid *Hustler*'s jokes are—even to find a pun is rare.) It's also still true that obscene jokes and pornographic images are only perceived by *some* women as an act of aggression against women, not by all, and individual "properness"—one index of class identification—is certainly a factor in how offended you get at a dirty joke or image.

This displeasure over pornography regularly gets expressed by feminists in the argument that pornography is dangerous to women. Or in statements like Andrea Dworkin's that "any violation of a woman's body can become sex for men; this is the essential truth of pornography."[20] But consider just how close these "danger arguments" are to what Mary Douglas calls "danger beliefs." These are all the ways that members of a society exhort each other into good citizenship by deploying predictions of disaster to enforce certain moral codes and social rules. In this kind of cosmology, centered on threats and fear, physical disasters or dangerous diseases are said to result from bad moral conduct—one sort of disease is caused by adultery, another by incest, and so on. Sexual dangers are a crucial part of this cosmology, with pollution fears, as we'll see, never very far away. According to Douglas's fieldwork, gender plays an important symbolic role in the realm of purity rituals and pollution violations: what it means is a way of symbolizing issues of social hierarchy.

> I believe that some pollutions are used as analogies for expressing a general view of the social order. For example, there are beliefs that each sex is a danger to the other through *contact with sexual fluids* [my emphasis]. . . . Such patterns of sexual danger can be seen to express symmetry or hierarchy. It is implausible to interpret them as expressing something about the actual relation of the sexes. I suggest that many ideas about sexual dangers are better interpreted as symbols of the relation between parts of society, as mirroring designs of hierarchy or symmetry which apply in the larger social system.[21]

Compare Douglas's comments on danger beliefs focused on "sexual fluids" to another passage by Andrea Dworkin: "In literary pornography, to ejaculate is to *pollute* the woman" (her emphasis). Dworkin goes on to discuss, in a lengthy excursus on semen, the collaboration between women-hating women's magazines, which "sometimes recommend spreading semen on the face to enhance the complexion" and pornography, where ejaculation often occurs on the woman's body or face: both, she writes, force women to accept semen and eroticize it. Her point seems to be that men *prefer* that semen be seen as disgusting, because the only way they can get sexual pleasure is through violation. Thus semen is "driven into [the woman] to dirty her or make her more dirty or make her dirty by him"; at the same time, semen has to be eroticized to get the woman to comply in her own violation.[22] That Dworkin sees contact with male "sexual fluids" as harmful to women is clear, as is the relation between pollution (again, it's Dworkin's own word) and ways of symbolizing danger beliefs.

For while it's true that *some* men *sometimes* pose sexual danger to women, the content of pollution beliefs, like Dworkin's analysis of pornography, expresses that danger symbolically at best: as anthropologist Douglas tells us, it's simply not plausible to take the content of these beliefs literally. In the Dworkin cosmology, there's a magical leap from the fact that "some men are violent" to "semen is dangerous," paralleling the equally problematic magical leap from the possibility that some rapists may look at pornography to the conclusion that pornography causes rape. A real fear, rape, finds expression in a symbolic and imaginary cause: pornography.

Historically, female reformism aimed at bettering the position of women has often had an unfortunately conservative social thrust. The temperance movement is a prime example, with the local interests of women in reforming rowdy or irresponsible male behavior too easily dovetailing with the interests of capital and officialdom in maintaining a passive, sober, and obedient work force. Although *Hustler*'s attacks on feminism might be seen simply as a backlash against the feminist second wave, they can also be seen as a political response to the conservatism of feminist calls for reform of the male imagination. There's no doubt that *Hustler* sees itself as doing battle with feminists: Gloria Steinem makes frequent appearances in the pages of the magazine as an uptight, and predictably upper-class, bitch. From

Hustler's point of view, feminism is an upper-class movement dedicated to annihilating the low-rent *Hustler* male and his pleasures. Resisting is a nascent form of class consciousness. To acquiesce to feminist insistence on the reform of the male imagination would be to identify upward along the social hierarchy—anathema to *Hustler*'s politics and ideology.

What precisely does it mean to be offended by pornography? And what does it mean to be offended *as women* by pornography?

Freud's view of the difference between the sexes is that little boys and girls are, at an early stage, both just as "interested" in sex. As each mature, part of the process of sexual differentiation is the increasing level of inhibition that girls and women inherit as part of the acquisition of femininity. Women end up, generally speaking, the more afflicted by sexual repression, according to Freud. This is actually pretty similar to *Hustler*'s view: repression is a social process that produces differing levels of inhibition, displeasure, or sexual interest between at least some men and some women. Antipornography feminists (along with the Christian right) tend to take the opposite position, rejecting a social-constructionist argument like Freud's in favor of a description of female sexuality as inborn and biologically based—something akin to the "normal human sensuality" Robin Morgan referred to.[23]

So a woman's discomfort at the dirty joke, and by extension, at pornography, is actually twofold. There's her discomfort at the intended violation, at being assailed, as Freud puts it, "with the part of the body or the procedure in question." But at the same time, what she's assailed with is the fact of her own repression (which isn't inborn or natural, according to Freud and *Hustler*, but acquired). Pornography's net effect (and perhaps its intent) is to unsettle a woman in her subjectivity, to point out that any "naturalness" of female sexuality and subjectivity of the sort that Morgan and many other feminists propagate isn't nature at all, but culture: part of the woman's own long-buried prehistory. A Freudian might add that what intensifies women's disgust at pornography is the unconscious renunciation of any residue of that early, pre-Oedipal "interest" in sex that little boys and little girls once shared. The classic Freudian example of a reaction-formation is a housewife whose obsession with cleanliness stems from a repressed interest in what's not "clean" (that is, sex), an obsession that actually allows her to focus all her attention on dust and dirt, thus affecting virtue and purity while coming close to satisfying the opposing, unacceptable instinct.[24] An antipornography crusader might be another such example: waging a fight against pornography means, in effect, spending most of your time looking at it and talking about it, while projecting the dirty interest onto others.

In addition, there's certainly a level of discomfort, for women, with the social fact of differences *between* women— that is, with other women's sexuality. After all, not all women *do* feel violated by male pornography, a fact that argues pretty convincingly against any account of female sexuality as uniform and natural. The antiporn rejoinder to this very real difference is to label those sisters "coerced," "brainwashed," or "male-identified," resolutely attempting to force onto all of us this singular version of inborn femininity, which is somehow less inborn in some of us than in others.

So pornography sets up a force field of disturbances around the thorny question of female subjectivity, and the even thornier question of the origins of sexual differences between men and women. After all, what does *Hustler*-variety porn consist of but some sort of male fantasy of women whose sexual desires are in perfect unison with men's? The male fantasy of female sexual willingness is perceived by some women as doing violence to their very beings. But the violence here is that of being mis-identified, of having one's desire misfigured as "male desire." I can easily feel offended at (my fantasy of) some disgusting, hairy, belching *Hustler* male imagining me or some other hapless woman panting lustfully after his bloated body, and imagining that our greatest goal in life is to play geisha girl to his kinky and bizarre pleasures. On the other hand, maybe if men read more Harlequin Romances, they'd be similarly offended to find *their* desires so misfigured—romance novels having been aptly referred to as "pornography for women." Pornography forces social differences in our faces: not only class differences, not only differences between male and female sexuality, but the range of differences between *women*. Calling one version of sexuality "nature" and assigning it to all women is false in many ways, not least of which involves turning an historically specific class and educational position—coincidentally, that of the femi-nist antiporn intellectual—into a universal that tramples over the existence of very real divisions between women.

Any automatic assumptions about *Hustler*-variety porn aiding and abetting the entrenchment of male power will be put into question by reading the magazine, which few of its critics man-age to do. *Hustler* itself often seems quite dubious about the status of men, wry and frequently perplexed about male and female sexual incompatability. On the one hand it offers the standard men's magazine fantasy bimbette: always ready, always horny, willing to do anything, and who inexplicably finds the *Hustler* male simply irresistible. But just as often there's her flip side: the woman disgusted by the *Hustler* male's desires and sexuality, a haughty, superior, rejecting, upper-class bitch-goddess. Class resentment is modulated through resentment of women's power to humiliate and reject: "Beauty isn't everything, except to the bitch who's got it. You see her stalking the aisles of Cartier, stuffing her perfect face at exorbitant cuisineries, tooling her Jag along private-access coastline roads . . ."

Doesn't this reek of disenfranchisement rather than any certainty about male power over women? The fantasy life here is animated by cultural disempowerment in relation to a sexual caste system and a social class system. This magazine is tinged with frustrated desire and rejection: *Hustler* gives vent to a vision of sex in which sex is an arena for failure and humiliation, rather than domination and power. Numerous ads play off male anxieties and feelings of inadequacy: various sorts of penis enlargers ("Here is your chance to overcome the problems and insecurities of a penis that is too small. Gain self-confidence and your ability to satisfy women will sky rocket" reads a typical ad), penis extenders, and erection aids (Stay-Up, Sta-Hard, etc.).[25] One of the problems with most porn is that men arrogate the power and privilege of having public fantasies about women's bodies without any risk or comparable exposure of the male body, which is invariably produced as powerful and inviolable. But *Hustler* does put the male body at risk, rehearsing and never completely alleviating male anxiety. And there's a surprising amount of castration humor in *Hustler,* as well.

Rejecting the compensatory fantasy life mobilized by *Playboy* and *Penthouse,* in which all women are willing and all men are studs—as long as its readers fantasize and identify upward, with money, power, good looks, and consumer durables—*Hustler* pulls the window dressing off the market/exchange nature of sexual romance: the market in attractiveness, the exchange basis of male-female relations in a society where men typically have more social and earning power than women. Sexual exchange is a frequent joke topic: women students are coerced into having sex with professors for grades, women are fooled into having sex by various ruses, lies, or barters engineered by males in power positions—bosses, doctors, and the like. All this is probably truer than not, but problematic from the standpoint of male fantasy. Power, deep pockets, and social prestige are represented as essential to sexual success, but the magazine works to disparage and oppose identification with these attributes on every front. The ways in which sex, gender, class, and power intersect in *Hustler* are complex, contradictory, unpredictable, and ambivalent, making it impossible to maintain that this is any simple exercise in male domination.

Much of *Hustler*'s humor is also manifestly political, devoted to dismantling abuses of political power and official privilege. A 1989 satirical photo feature titled "Farewell to Reagan: Ronnie's Last Bash" highlights just how the magazine's standard repertoire of aesthetic techniques—nudity, grossness, and offense to the conventions of polite society—can be directly translated into scathingly effective political language. The pornographic idiom is quite explicitly deployed as a form of political speech, one that refuses to buy into the pompously serious and high-minded language that high culture considers appropriate to political discourse. Here *Hustler* thumbs its nose at both dominant culture's politics *and* its language.

The photo spread, laid out like a series of black and white surveillance photos, begins with this no-words-minced introduction:

> It's been a great eight years—for the power elite, that is. You can bet Nancy planned long and hard how to celebrate Ron Reagan's successful term of filling special-interest coffers while fucking John Q. Citizen right up the yazoo. A radical tax plan that more than halved taxes for the rich while doubling the working man's load; detaxation of in-

dustries, who trickled down their windfalls into mergers, takeovers, and investments in foreign lands; crooked deals with enemies of U.S. allies in return for dirty money for right wing killers to reclaim former U.S. business territories overseas; more than 100 appointees who resigned in disgrace over ethics or outright criminal charges . . . are all the legacies of the Reagan years . . . and we'll still get whiffs of bullyboy Ed Meese's sexual intimidation policies for years to come, particularly with conservative whores posing as Supreme Court justices.

The photos that follow are of an elaborately staged orgiastic White House farewell party, with the appropriate motley faces of the eighties political elite photomontaged onto naked and seminaked bodies doing obscene things to one another. (The warning "Parody: Not to be taken seriously. Celebrity heads stripped onto our model's bodies" accompanies each and every photo, a concession to *Hustler*'s legal travails.) That more of the naked bodies are female and that many are in what might be described as a service relation to male bodies opens up the possibility of misogyny charges. But what becomes problematic for such a singular reading is that within the parody, the imaginary staging of the rituals of male sexual power functions in favor of an overtly political critique.

The style is like a *Mad* magazine cartoon come to life with a multiplication of detail in every shot: the Ted Kennedy dartboard in one corner; in another, stickers that exhort "Invest in South Africa"; the plaque over Reagan's bed announcing "Joseph McCarthy slept here." In the main room of the party, various half-naked women cavort, Edwin Meese is glimpsed filching a candelabra. Reagan greets a hooded Ku Klux Klanner at the door, and a helpful caption translates the action: "Ron tells an embarrassed Jesse Helms it wasn't a come-as-you-are party." In the background the corpse of deceased CIA chief Bill Casey watches benignly over the proceedings (his gaping mouth doubles as an ashtray), as does former press secretary James Brady—the victim of John Hinckley's assassination attempt and Reagan's no-gun-control policy—who, propped in a wheelchair, wears a sign bluntly announcing "Vegetable Dip" around his neck.

In the next room Oliver North, cast as a musclebound male stripper, gyrates on top of a table, while the fawning figures of Iran-Contra coconspirators Poindexter, Secord, and Weinberger are gathered at his feet, stuffing dollar bills into his G-string holster in homoerotic reverie. Next we come upon Jerry Falwell, masturbating to a copy of *Hustler* concealed in his Bible, a bottle of Campari at his bedside and an "I love Mom" button pinned to his jacket (this a triumphant post–libel suit *Hustler* pouring salt on the wound). In yet another bedroom, "former Democrat and supreme skagbait Jeane Kirkpatrick demonstrates why she switched to the Republican Party" as, grinning and topless, we find her on the verge of anally penetrating a bespectacled George Bush with the dildo attached to her ammunition belt. A whiny Elliott Abrams, pants around his ankles and dick in hand, tries unsuccessfully to pay off a prostitute who won't have him; the naked Pat Robertson, doggie style on the bed, is being disciplined by a naked angel with a cat-o'-nine-tails. And on the last page the invoice to the American citizen: $283 million.

While the antiestablishment politics of this photo spread are pretty clear, *Hustler* can also be maddeningly incoherent, marauding all over what we usually think of as the political spectrum. *Hustler*'s development of the pornographic idiom as a political form may make it politically troublesome if you're coming from the old world of traditional political alliances and oppositions: right-left, misogynist-feminist. And it may be just these traditional political meanings that *Hustler* throws into question, along with the whole question of what misogyny means.

It's true that many women feel assaulted and affronted by *Hustler*'s images. But it's also true that *Hustler*'s use of nudity is often political: it's clear in "Reagan's Farewell Party" that nudity is deployed as a leveling device, a deflating technique following a long tradition of political satire. This puts another of *Hustler*'s scandals—its notorious nude photo spread of Jackie Onassis, captured sunbathing on her Greek island, Skorpios, by telephoto lens—in a different and perhaps more subversive light.

Feminists regarded this as simply another case of *Hustler*'s misogyny, but the strategic uses of nudity we've seen elsewhere in the magazine indicate something else entirely: not Onassis as unwilling sexual object, but Onassis as political target. Nudity is used throughout the magazine as an attack on the life-styles of the rich, famous, and politically powerful—Reagan, North, Falwell, Abrams, Kirkpatrick, and in another feature, Thatcher, all (unfortunately for the squeamish) *sans* clothes. This makes it difficult to argue that Onassis's nudity functions strictly in relation to her sex, exploiting women's vulnerability as a class, or that its message can be reduced to a genericizing one like "You may be rich but you're just a cunt like any other cunt." Rather, Jackie Onassis's appearance on the pages of *Hustler* forces to our attention what might be called the sexual caste system, and these connections between sex and caste make it difficult to come to easy moral conclusions about *Hustler*'s violation of Onassis's privacy.

As various pulp biographies inform us, the Bouvier sisters, Jacqueline and Princess Lee, were more or less bred to take up positions as consorts of rich and powerful men. To, one might put it bluntly, professionally deploy their femininity. This isn't so very unlike the case of *Hustler*'s somewhat less privileged, consenting models, who while engaged in a similar activity are confined to very different social locales and addresses. Some of these are portrayed in a regular *Hustler* feature, "The Beaver

Hunt," a photo gallery of snapshots of nonprofessional models sent in by readers.[26]

Posed in paneled rec rooms, on plaid Sears sofas or cheap chenille bedspreads, draped amidst the kind of matching bedroom suites seen on late-night easy-credit furniture ads, nude or in Victoria's Secret lingerie, they're identified as secretaries, waitresses, housewives, nurses, bank tellers, cosmetology students, cashiers, factory workers, saleswomen, data processors, and nurse's aides. Without generalizing from this insufficient data about any kind of *typical* class differences about appropriate or inappropriate displays of the body, we might simply ask, so where are all the doctors, lawyers, corporate execs, and college professors? Or moving up the social hierarchy, where are the socialites, the jet setters, the wives of CEOs? Absent because of their fervent feminism? Probably not. Isn't it because they've struck—or were born into—a better deal?[27]

By placing the snapshots of Onassis in the place of the cashier, the secretary, and the waitress, *Hustler* performs another upheaval, violating all the rigid social distinctions that our classless society claims it doesn't make, and violating those spatial boundaries (like private islands) that the rich are able to purchase to protect themselves from the hordes. These are precisely the kinds of unconscious distinctions we *all* make that allow us to regard the deployment of femininity that achieves marriage to a billionaire shipping magnate as a very different thing from the one that lands you an honorary spot in this month's "Beaver Hunt."

The political implications of the Onassis photo spread demonstrate the need for a vastly more complex approach to the question of misogyny than those currently circulating. If any symbolic exposure or violation of *any* woman's body is regarded by feminists as simply a byproduct of the misogynistic male imagination, we overlook the fact that not all women, simply by virtue of being women, are allies. Women can both symbolize and exercise class power and privilege, not to mention oppressive political power. (And thanks to equal opportunity employment, even wage pointless neoimperialist wars.)

Hustler's "violations" are *symbolic*. Treating images of staged sex or violence as equivalent to real sex or violence, or cynically trying to convince us that it's a direct line from sexual imagery to rape—as if merely looking at images of sex magically brainwashes any man into becoming a robotic sexual plunderer—will clearly restrict political expression and narrow the forms of political discourse. Given the pervasiveness of real violence against women, it's understandable to want to pin it on something so easily at hand as sexual representation. But this mistakes being offended for being endangered, and they're not the same thing. Pornography makes an easy target for all manner of social anxieties, but the bad consequences for both feminism and democracy make this a dangerously insufficient tactic.

On the other hand, *Hustler* is certainly not politically unproblematic. While it may be radical in its refusal of bourgeois proprieties, its transgressiveness has limits, and its refusal of polite speech in areas of social sensitivity—AIDS or race, for example—doesn't automatically guarantee any kind of countercultural force. Although frequently accused of racism, *Hustler* basically just wants to offend anyone, of any race, any ethnic group. Not content to offend only the Right, it makes doubly sure to offend liberals; not content merely to taunt whites, it hectors blacks and other minorities. Its favored tactic with regard to race is simply to reproduce every stereotype it can think of: the subject of most *Hustler* cartoons featuring blacks will invariably be huge sexual organs that every woman lusts after, alternating with black watermelon-eating lawbreakers. *Hustler's* letter columns carry out a raging debate on the subject of race, with

black readers writing variously that they find *Hustler*'s irrever-
ence funny or resent its stereotypes, whites either applauding
or protesting. (And it's clear that the most explicitly political
forms of popular culture these days—rap music, for example—
are ones that also refuse polite speech.)

If publisher Larry Flynt, who has been regularly accused of racism, was indeed shot by white supremacist Joseph Paul Franklin,
who is serving two life sentences for racially motivated killings
(and who has claimed responsibility for the shooting), this is yet
another twist in the strange and contradictory tale of *Hustler*'s
curious impact on American culture. Larry Flynt's swaggering
determination to parade the contents of his private obsessions
as public psychodrama in the courtrooms and headlines of the
nation—not so unlike other "larger-than-life" figures who spo-
radically capture the public imagination—is just one element
in a life story replete with all the elements of epic drama. (So it
comes as no surprise that the equally swaggering director Oliver
Stone is producing a bio-pic on Flynt's life.) The Flynt biography
is nothing short of a morality tale for our times: a late-twentieth-
century pornographic Horatio Alger who comes to suffer horribly
for his ambitions, despite his frantic, futile gestures of repentance.
　　Shortly before the 1978 shooting, at the height of both
Hustler's circulation and his own near-universal excoriation,
Flynt undertook one of those elaborate acts of self-reinvention
that are so deeply American, given our national legacy of Puri-
tan conversion narratives and self-refashioning: he underwent
a highly publicized conversion to evangelical Christianity at the
hands of presidential sister Ruth Carter Stapleton. The two were
pictured chastely hand in hand as Flynt announced plans to turn
Hustler into a *religious* skin magazine and told a Pentecostal
congregation in Houston (where he was attending the National

Women's Conference), "I owe every woman in America an apology." He was apparently sincere, and announced plans to reincarnate the "Asshole of the Month" as "Turkey of the Month," and to convert the unsavory cartoon character "Chester the Molester" into the more benign "Chester the Protector," whose mission would be protecting young girls from corruption. Flynt became celibate (he claimed) and a vegetarian, in an attempt to "purify himself." Ironically, it was this very religious conversion that led to the notorious *Hustler* cover of a woman being ground up in a meat grinder, which was, according to insiders, a sheepish and flat-footed attempt at an another public apology by Flynt to women at large. ("We will no longer hang women up as pieces of meat" was the widely ignored caption to the photo. Recall here Freud's observation on the sophistication of the joke form as a class trait.[28]) Flynt proclaimed, "It's not a publicity stunt. I have asked God for forgiveness for anything I have done to hurt anyone. I've been all the way to the bottom. There's only one way to go now, and that's up. I'm going to be hustling for the Lord." (Wife Althea, the practical half of the couple, commented, "God may have walked into your life, but twenty million dollars just walked out.")

But it was not to be. There was another fate in store for Larry Flynt, and one less convert for the Lord: Flynt renounced religion shortly after the shooting. In one of the many ironies of this all-too ironic story, one which would seem absurd in the most hackneyed piece of fiction, the man who raked in millions on the fantasy of endlessly available fucking is now left impotent. And in 1982, after four years of constant pain, the nerves leading to his legs were cauterized to stop all sensation: Flynt, who built an empire offending bourgeois sensibilities with their horror of errant bodily functions, is left with no bowel or urinary control. Some God with a cruel and over-developed sense of irony seems to have authored the second act. And while the Flynt empire is now a hugely profitable conglomerate, publishing mainstream rags like *Maternity Fashion and Beauty* (and distributing numerous others, including the intellectually tony *New York Review of Books*), Larry Flynt lately devotes his days to collecting antiques, finally adopting the pastimes of the leisure classes into which his talent for vulgarity allowed him entrée.[29]

Flynt's obsessional one-man war against all public and private constraints on the body made him evil personified to the government, the church, and feminists. Yet willingly or not, Flynt's own body has been on the line as well. In this case the pornographer's body has borne, full force, the violent reprisals aimed at those who transgress our most deeply venerated social boundaries and bodily proprieties.

Five

How to Look
at Pornography

Pornography grabs us and doesn't let go. Whether you're revolted or enticed, shocked or titillated, these are flip sides of the same response: an intense, visceral engagement with what pornography has to say. And pornography has quite a lot to say. Pornography should interest us, because it's intensely and relentlessly *about* us. It involves the roots of our culture and the deepest corners of the self. It's not just friction and naked bodies: pornography has eloquence. It has meaning, it has ideas. It even has redeeming ideas. So what's everyone so wrought up about?

Maybe it's that buried under all the nervous stereotypes of pimply teenagers, furtive perverts in raincoats, and asocial compulsively masturbating misfits, beneath all these disdainful images of the lone pornography consumer, is a certain sneaking recognition that pornography isn't just an individual predilection: pornography is central to our culture. I'm not simply referring to its immense popularity (although estimates put its sales at over \$11 billion a year). I mean that pornography is revealing, and what it reveals isn't just a lot of naked people sweating on each other. It exposes the culture to itself. Pornography is the royal road to the cultural psyche (as for Freud, dreams were the route to the unconscious). So the question is, if you put it on the couch and let it free-associate, what is it really saying? What are the inner tensions and unconscious conflicts that propel its narratives?

Popularity doesn't tell you everything, but it can tell you a lot. Like the Hollywood blockbuster or other cultural spectacles, what transforms a collection of isolated strangers with different lives, interests, and idiosyncrasies into a mass audience is that elusive "thing" that taps into the culture's attention, often before it's even aware that that's where its preoccupations and anxieties are located. Audiences constitute themselves around things that matter to them, and stay away in droves when no nerve is struck. Behind mass cultural spectacles from *Jurassic Park* to Ross Perot to the O. J. Simpson trial or any other spectator attraction, what commands our attention, our bucks, our votes are the things that get under our skin, that condense and articulate what matters to us. I want to suggest however, perhaps somewhat perversely, that the endless attention pornography commands, whether from its consumers *or* its protesters (who are, if anything, even more obsessed by pornography than those who use it), has less to do with its obvious content (sex) than with what might be called its political philosophy.

When writing about the pornography of the past, whether visual or literary, scholars and art historians routinely uncover allegorical meanings within it, even political significance. The question of how its content relates to its social moment and historical context supersedes questions about whether it should or shouldn't have existed, or how best to protect the public from offense to their sensibilities. Historians have made the case that modern pornography (up until around the nineteenth century) operated against political and religious authority as a form of social criticism, a vehicle for attacking officialdom, which responded, predictably, by attempting to suppress it. Pornography was defined less by its content than by the efforts of those in power to eliminate it and whatever social agendas it transported.[1]

Even knowing this, it seems quite impossible to begin to think about contemporary pornography as a form of culture, or as a mode of politics. There's zero discussion of pornography as an expressive medium in the positive sense—the only expressing it's presumed to do is of misogyny or social decay. That it might have more complicated social agendas, or that future historians of the genre might generate interesting insights about pornography's relation to this particular historical and social moment—these are radically unthought thoughts. One reason for this lacuna is a certain intellectual prejudice against taking porn seriously at all. Those who take pornography seriously are its opponents, who have little interesting to say on the subject: not only don't they seem to have spent much time actually looking at it, but even worse, they seem universally overcome by a leaden, stultifying literalness, apparently never having heard of metaphor, irony, a symbol—even fantasy seems too challenging a concept.

I've proposed that pornography is both a legitimate form of culture and a fictional, fantastical, even allegorical realm; it neither simply reflects the real world nor is it some hypnotizing call to action. The world of pornography is mythological and hyperbolic, peopled by characters. It doesn't and never will exist, but it does—and this is part of its politics—insist on a sanctioned space for fantasy. This is its most serious demand and the basis of much of the controversy it engenders, because pornography has a talent for making its particular fantasies look like dangerous and socially destabilizing incendiary devices.

Sweating naked bodies and improbable sexual acrobatics

are only one side of the story. The other is the way pornography holds us in the thrall of its theatrics of transgression, its dedication to crossing boundaries and violating social strictures. Like any other popular-culture genre (sci-fi, romance, mystery, true crime), pornography obeys certain rules, and its primary rule is transgression. Like your boorish cousin, its greatest pleasure is to locate each and every one of society's taboos, prohibitions, and proprieties and systematically transgress them, one by one.

As the avant-garde knew, transgression is no simple thing: it's a precisely calculated intellectual endeavor. It means knowing the culture inside out, discerning its secret shames and grubby secrets, and knowing how to best humiliate it, knock it off its prim perch. (To commit sacrilege, you have to have studied the religion.) A culture's pornography becomes, in effect, a very precise map of that culture's borders: pornography begins at the edge of the culture's decorum. Carefully tracing that edge, like an anthropologist mapping a culture's system of taboos and myths, gives you a detailed blueprint of the culture's anxieties, investments, contradictions. And a culture's borders, whether geographical or psychological, are inevitably political questions —as mapmakers and geographers are increasingly aware.

Pornography is also a form of political theater. Within the incipient, transgressive space opened by its festival of social infractions is a medium for confronting its audiences with exactly those contents that are exiled from sanctioned speech, from mainstream culture and political discourse. And that encompasses more than sex. Our legacy of Puritanism makes sex a vehicle for almost anything subject to repression and shame: sex becomes a natural home for all forms of rebellion, utopianism, flaunting, or experimentation. Like adolescents who "use" sex to express their rebellion, anything banished from social sanction can hitch its wagon to sex and use pornography as a backdoor form of cultural entrée. (Of course, that any kind of social rebellion is instantly dismissed as adolescent is indicative of how shaming and silencing tactics are employed to banish a vast range of meanings. Which is precisely why pornography becomes such a useful vehicle for hurtling those meanings back into view.) Pornography has many uses beyond the classic one-handed one.

Like the avant-garde's, pornography's transgressions are first of all aesthetic. It confronts us with bodies that repulse us—like fat ones—or defies us with genders we find noxious. It induces us to look at what's conventionally banished from view. Pornography is chock full of these sorts of aesthetic shocks and surprises. Here's another one: in a culture that so ferociously equates sexuality with youth, where else but within pornography will you find enthusiasm for sagging, aging bodies, *or* for their sexualization? There is indeed a subgenre of porn—both gay and straight—devoted to the geriatric. The degree of one's aesthetic distress when thumbing through magazines with titles like *40+*, with its wrinkly models and not-so-perky breasts, or *Over 50,* with its naked pictorials of sagging white-haired grandmothers (or the white-haired grandfathers of *Classics*, with their big bellies and vanishing hairlines, and, turning the page, the two lumbering CEOs in bifocals and boxer shorts fondling each other), indicates the degree to which a socially prescribed set of aesthetic conventions is embedded in the very core of our beings. And our sexualities.

It also indicates the degree to which pornography exists precisely to pester and thwart the dominant. The vistas of antediluvian flesh in *Over 50,* or its features like "Promiscuous Granny," counter all of the mainstream culture's stipulations regarding sex and sexual aesthetics. One may want to argue that these subgenres of pornography simply cater to "individual preferences" or to dismiss them as "perversions," depending on how far you carry your normativity. But for the individual viewer, it's not just a case of different strokes for different folks. Pornography provides a realm of transgression that is, in effect, a counter-aesthetics to dominant norms for bodies, sexualities, and desire itself. And to the extent that portraying the aging body as sexual might be dissed as a perversion (along with other "perversions" like preferring fat sex partners), it reveals to what extent "perversion" is a shifting and capricious social category, rather than a form of knowledge or science: a couple of hundred years ago, fat bodies were widely admired.

Why a specific individual has this or that sexual preference isn't my concern here, in the same way that why Mr. Jones is or isn't a sci-fi fan isn't the concern of a popular-culture critic. What the cultural critic wants to account for is the "why" behind forms of fandom, and behind the existence of particular genres of popular culture, and to distill from them the knowledge they impart about the social: she might say, for example, that sci-fi is a genre in which anxieties about human possibilities in the context of expanding science and out-of-control technologies can be narratively articulated. We know, or learn, certain things about ourselves because we find them registered in our cultural forms. So too with the existence of these variegations within pornography. What shapes these subgenres—their content, their raw materials—are precisely the items blackballed from the rest of culture. This watchfully dialectical relation pornography maintains to mainstream culture makes it nothing less than a form of cultural critique. It refuses to let us so easily off the hook for our hypocrisies. Or our unconsciouses.

The edges of culture are exquisitely threatening places. Straddling them gives you a very different vantage point on things. Maybe it makes us a little nervous. (And what makes us nervous makes us conservative and self-protective.) Crossing that edge is an intense border experience of pleasure and danger, arousal and outrage—because these edges aren't only cultural: they're the limits that define us as individuals. We don't *choose* the social codes we live by, they choose us. Pornography's very specific, very calculated violations of these strict codes (which have been pounded into all of us from the crib) make it the exciting and the nerve-wracking thing it is. These are the limits we yearn to defy and transcend—some of us more than others, apparently. (And of course taboos function to stimulate the desire for the tabooed thing *and* for its prohibition simultaneously.)

The danger and thrill of social transgression can be profoundly gratifying or profoundly distasteful, but one way or another, pornography, by definition, leaves no social being unaffected. Why? Because pornography's very preoccupation with the instabilities and permeability of cultural borders is inextricable from the fragility and tenuousness of our own psychic borders, composed as they are of this same flimsy system of refusals and repressions. Pornography's allegories of transgression reveal, in the most visceral ways, not only our culture's edges, but how intricately our own identities are bound up in all of these quite unspoken, but quite relentless, cultural dictates. And what the furor over pornography also reveals is just how deeply attached to the most pervasive feelings of shame and desire all these unspoken dictates are. Pornography's ultimate desire is exactly to engage our deepest embarrassments, to mock us for the anxious psychic balancing acts we daily perform, straddling between the anarchy of sexual desires and the straitjacket of social responsibilities.

Pornography, then, is profoundly and paradoxically social, but even more than that, it's acutely historical. It's an archive of data about both our history as a culture and our own individual histories—our formations as selves. Pornography's favorite terrain is the tender spots where the individual psyche collides with the historical process of molding social subjects.

This may have something to do with the great desire so

many pornography commentators have to so vastly *undercompli-cate* the issue, to studiously ignore the meanings that frame and underlie all the humping and moaning. It's as if they're so distracted by naked flesh that anything beyond the superficial becomes unreadable, like watching a movie and only noticing the celluloid, or going to the revolution and only noticing the costumes. It is not *just* sex, *just* violence, *just* a question of First Amendment protection. It's exactly because the experience of pornography is so intensely complicated and fraught with all the complications of personhood, in addition to all the complications of gendered personhood, that pornography is so aggravating. It threatens and titillates because it bothers those fragile places. It tickles our sensitive spots. Tickling is in fact one of the categories of pornography that's particularly interesting in this regard. Why *is* there a variety of pornography devoted to the experience of tickling, being tickled, and, especially, being tickled against one's will?

Of course, neither the culture nor the individual have had their particular borders for very long. These aren't timeless universals. The line between childhood and adulthood, standards of privacy, bodily aesthetics, and proprieties, our ideas about whom we should have sex with, and how to do it—*all* the motifs that obsess pornography—shift from culture to culture and throughout history.

The precondition for pornography is a civilizing process whose instruments are shame and repression. One of pornography's large themes is that we're adults who were once children, in whom the social has been instilled at great and often tragic cost. (And by definition incompletely, if you follow the Freudian understanding of the unconscious as a warehouse for everything that's repressed in the process of becoming a social being—for example, wanting to fuck your parents.) Of course, one major thing our society doesn't want to contemplate in any way, shape, or form is childhood sexuality. If you regard pornography in these somewhat more complicated terms (that is, if you start out from the presupposition that it *has* cultural complexity), then many of its more exotic subgenres may start to seem a little less peculiar, particularly since so many of them—from your standard bondage and dominance to the slightly more kinky terrain of spanking and punishment, to the outer frontiers of diapers and infantilism—seem such evident, belated, poignant memorials to the erotics of childhood.

In *Strictly Spanking*, an array of fairly ordinary-looking men and women get what's coming to them, and good. The spanker is always a woman. (Mother-dominated child-rearing *is* the norm in our society.) A frilly yellow dress is hiked up to reveal the red flush of recently spanked buttocks; a scary Joan Crawford–ish suburban matriarch is poised to do some serious damage to your posterior with the business end of a hairbrush; you're forced to bend over a pillow and get a good thrashing for whatever naughty thing you did. The standard poses include naked and facing the corner, garments around the ankles, or bent over the disciplinarian's knee. Hairbrushes, paddles, and switches are the preferred disciplinary apparatuses. You've been bad and need to be punished. You can almost hear the running commentary under the soundtrack of rhythmic thwacking: "This hurts me more than it hurts you," "When will you ever learn?" "Clean up your goddamn room!" There's no particular mystery about the origin of the erotics of humiliation.[2]

I mentioned tickling. In "A Plume for the Pledge," the lead feature in the premiere issue of *Tickling,* we're introduced to Tess and Helen: "Tess waits patiently—though a bit on the nervous side. Helen, a junior, knows that a feather can hurt more than a paddle. . . . It's initiation time on campus. The pledges are going through Hell Week. Paddles have been outlawed, but the university authorities forgot that tickling can be the most excruciating form of punishment." Let's think about the tone of this for a minute—after all, it's not exactly high realism. There's a certain knowingness about the enterprise: the creation of a fantasy scenario with stock elements. Two interchangeable twentyish ponytailed blondes in white underwear inhabit the living room of Sorority House, USA. Helen holds the pledge's hands behind her back, tickling the bottoms of her feet mercilessly with feathers. Soon the underwear comes off, and the tickling continues. Twenty black-and-white pictures of the same two girls, the same scene, the same feather, with minor variations. A few closeups on feet. A rope is produced; now Tess is tied down—she doesn't seem to mind, though, she's laughing away. A few photos catch Helen looking a little pensive, maybe a bit melancholy, but she quickly returns to her usual fun-loving self and it's just another gigglefest at Delta Gamma.

What sort of homage is this? As psychoanalyst Adam Phillips points out, "A child will never be able to tickle himself. It is the pleasure he can't reproduce in the absence of the other. The exact spots of ticklishness require—are—the enacted recognition of the other. To tickle is above all to seduce, often by amusement."[3] For Phillips, this would seem to be something of a memorial to childhood seduction, but seduction in the sense that we all crave it: as a form of attention and recognition. And perhaps, in the case of tickling, one charged with erotics as well. It's this erotic component of childhood that's routinely censored and goes widely undiscussed. Phillips points out that psychoanalysis too is essentially a theory of censorship—a catalog of materials that are repressed and not allowed into consciousness. Pornography, which as we see covers quite a similar terrain (which is what makes psychoanalytic theory such a useful explanatory device for it), is similarly subject to the wrath of censors—both internal and state—border police both. Tickling is one of those permeable borders: between play and sex, between sadism and fun, certainly between adult and childhood sexuality.

This border between childhood and adulthood is both the most porous and the most zealously patrolled, which may be why a magazine like *Diapers* is so consternating—even though it's just a series of pictorials of a winsome young man, maybe late twenties, but dressed throughout in extra-large Pampers, rubber pants, and a succession of pretty bonnets and frocks. Speaking of censorship, it's interesting to note that when Freud's notorious quote, "Anatomy is destiny," is cited, it's invariably employed to refer to the differences between male and female sex organs, and to taunt Freud for his always-lurking misogyny. But Freud actually used this quote (a paraphrase from Napoleon) twice, and the other reference is to the psychological consequences of nature's weird decision to put the sex organs and elimination functions into the same "neighborhood," as Freud so charmingly puts it.[4] His point is that this proximity has a series of affective consequences: from the disgust that so often seeps over into sex to the child's sexual arousal during parental hygiene ministrations. There are certain things we just don't want to know about ourselves, and about our formations as selves. These seem to be precisely what pornography keeps shoving right back at us.

Well, if you want to go around in diapers, why not just do it in the privacy of your own home, or under your rock? Why do these people have to parade their squalid little obsessions in front of the rest of us? One reason is that pornography would be nowhere without its most flagrant border transgression, this complete disregard for the public/private divide. Flaunting its contempt for all the proprieties, it's this transgression in particular that triggers so much handwringing about the deleterious effects on society of naked private parts in public view. These deeply held standards of privacy of ours are, of course, relatively recent, historically speaking. They're a modern invention, tied to the rise of the middle class, the invention of the modern autonomous individual, and the consequent transformations of daily life into an elaborately complicated set of negotiations between body, psyche, and the social. Equally modern, and perhaps even more relevant, are the corresponding inventions of sexual and bodily functions as sites of shame and disgust, which arise simultaneously, around the early Renaissance, further fueling the necessity of privacy.[5]

But this public/private boundary is ever shifting. In fact, it's flip-flopping so fast these days it's hard to keep up, and it's precisely these shifts that form the subtext of so much else that's disturbing the cultural equilibrium: for example, the recent focus on the pervasiveness of incest and domestic violence, privacy rackets both. This question of privacy is by no means a simple one. Pornography is often cited, by antiporn feminists, as a causal factor in many bad things that happen to women. But the fact is, these domestic abuses depend completely on the protections of privacy (which is clearly not the Arcadia pornography's critics would have us believe), whereas pornography's impulse is in the reverse direction: toward exposure, toward making the private public and the hidden explicit. Given the kinds of power abuses that privacy so usefully shields, and the social changes that exposure can, at times, engender, the privacy/publicity opposition doesn't have any clear heroes.

What's often referred to as the tabloidization of American culture also reflects shifting standards of public and private. When lower-middle America takes to the airwaves to brandish the intimate details of their lives—their secret affairs, their marital skirmishes, their familial contretemps—and talk show guests duke it out on air, high-minded critics invariably respond with contemptuous little think pieces snorting about what bad taste this all is. But taste is a complicated issue, and the history of the concept is entirely bound up with issues of social class and class distinctions.[6] "Keeping things to yourself," the stiff upper lip, the suppression of emotions, maintenance of propriety and proper behavior, and the very concept of "bad taste" are all associated historically with the ascendancy of the bourgeoisie and their invention of behaviors that would separate themselves from the noisy lower orders. All of our impulses (and snobbery) about what should be private or what shouldn't be public are enormously complex, historically laden cultural machinery. Given that all these public/private dilemmas are intricately connected to governing affects of deep and overwhelming shame and embarrassment, our immediate impulses and our "taste" aren't always the most reliable indicators of anything but obedience to a shifting set of conventions, whose purposes we're constitutionally disinclined to question, as *Hustler* makes so clear.

This recent dedication to exposure and propriety violations, this "tabloid sensibility" that seems to now dominate American cultural life, may not be unrelated to the economic decline that has forced downward mobility down the throats of a once economically optimistic Middle America. If a lifetime of hard work is no longer any guarantee of financial security—of a home, or continued employment, or a pension—and if upward aspirations now look like so much nostalgia for earlier times, why adopt the deportment or the sensibility of the classes you can't afford to join? Class, after all, isn't simply a matter of income, or neighborhood. It's also embedded in a complex web of attitudes and proprieties, particularly around the body. (This is something "Roseanne" viewers know all about.)

Pornography, of course, dedicates itself to offending all the bodily and sexual proprieties intrinsic to upholding class distinctions: good manners, privacy, the absence of vulgarity, the suppression of bodily instincts into polite behavior. It's not only porn's theatrics of transgression that ensure its connotation of lowness, it's also pornography's relentless downward focus. This is one explanation for why pornography doesn't appear ripe for serious critical interpretation. Imagine culture as a class system, with the "top" of culture comprised of rarefied, pricey, big-ticket cultural forms like opera, serious theater, gallery art, the classics, the symphony, modernist literature. Moving down a bit you get your art-house and European films; down a bit more, public television, Andrew Lloyd Webber, and other middlebrow diversions. If you keep moving on down through the tiers of popular culture—down through teen-pics, soap operas, theme parks, tabloid TV, the *National Enquirer*, Elvis paintings on velvet— then right down at the very bottom rung of the ladder is pornography. It's the lowest of the cultural low, on perpetual standby to represent the nadir of culture, whenever some commentator needs a visible cultural sign to index society's moral turpitude.

But let's be honest about this cultural hierarchy. If pornography is at the bottom of a cultural class system whose apex comprises the forms of culture we usually think of as consumed by social elites with deep pockets—after all, take a look at the price of an opera ticket, or at the clothes at the opening night of the symphony—then questions of social class seem to lurk somewhere quite near all this distress over pornography. If culture is grouped along a hierarchy from high to low, and the rest of our social world is grouped along a hierarchy from high to low, then this puts pornography into analogy with the bottom tiers of the social structure. This isn't to suggest that the "lower classes" are pornography's consumers, but that insofar as porn is relegated to a low thing culturally, it takes on all the *associations* of a low-class thing.

Take the dual associations antipornography feminists make between pornography and violent male behavior. It hardly needs saying that the propensity to violence is a characteristic with strong class connotations—you might even say stereotypical connotations. A propensity to violence is in opposition to traits like rationality, contemplation, and intelligence, which tend to have higher-class connotations: the attributes associated with the audiences of higher cultural forms like theater or opera. The argument that pornography causes violent behavior in male consumers relies on a theory of the porn consumer as devoid of rationality, contemplation, or intelligence, prone instead to witless brainwashing, to monkey-see/monkey-do reenactments of the pornographic scene. This would be a porn spectator who inherently *has* a propensity to become violent (not presumably the members of the Meese Commission, who spent years viewing pornography without violent consequences). Maybe it becomes clearer how fantastical this argument is when you consider how eagerly we accept the premise that pornography causes violence—and are so keen to regulate it—compared to the massive social disinclination to accept that *handguns* cause violence (and it's certainly far more provable that they do): guns, without the same connotation of lowness, don't seem to invite the same regulatory zeal, despite a completely demonstrable causal relation to violence.[7]

The fantasy pornography consumer is a walking projection of upper-class fears about lower-class men: brutish, animal-like, sexually voracious. And this fantasy is projected back onto pornography. In fact, arguments about the "effects" of culture seem to be applied exclusively to lower cultural forms, that is to pornography, or cartoons, or subcultural forms like gangsta rap. This predisposition even extends to social science research: researchers aren't busy wiring Shakespeare viewers up to electrodes and measuring their penile tumescence or their galvanic skin responses to the violence or misogyny there. The violence of high culture seems not to have effects on *its* consumers, or rather, no one bothers to research this question, so we don't hear much about how *Taming of the Shrew* expresses contempt for women, or watching *Medea* might compel a mother to go out and kill her children; when a South Carolina mother did recently drown her two kids, no one suggested banning Euripides. When Lorena Bobbitt severed husband John's penis, no one wondered if she'd recently watched Oshima's *In the Realm of the Senses*, the Japanese art film where a male character meets a similar bloody fate. Is that because the audiences of Euripides and Oshima have greater self-control than the audiences of pornography and other low culture, or is this a class prejudice that masquerades as the "redeeming social value" issue?

The presumption that low cultural forms are without complexity is completely embedded in media effects research. I was quite startled to read that one of the country's leading pornography researchers routinely screens the notorious sexploitation movie *I Spit on Your Grave* as an example of sexual violence against women, then measures male audiences for mood, hostility, and desensitization to rape.[8] But as anyone who's actually seen this movie knows, it's no simple testimonial to rape. This is a rape-*revenge* film, in which a female rape victim wreaks violent reprisal against her rapists, systematically and imaginatively killing all three, and one mentally challenged onlooker—by decapitation, hanging, shooting, and castration. Film theorist Carol Clover, who does see low culture as having complexity, points out that even during the rape sequence, the camera angles force the viewer into identification with the female victim.[9] If male college students are hostile after watching this movie (with its grisly castration scene), who knows *what* it is they're actually reacting to? Antiporn activists are fond of throwing around data from social science research to support the contention that pornography leads to violence, but this research is so shot through with simplistic assumptions about its own materials that it seems far from clear what's even being measured. (Or how it's being measured: data collection in sex research based on sexual self-reporting is so frequently unreliable and plagued with discrepancies that researchers resort to cooking the numbers to make them make sense: the general population apparently doesn't report on its sexual experiences in ways that translate into neat statistical columns.[10])

If pornography too is laden with complexity and meaning, and even "redeeming value," then the presumption that only low culture causes "effects" starts to look more and more like a stereotype about its imagined viewers and their intelligence, or their self-control, or their values. Pornography isn't viewed as having complexity, because its *audience* isn't viewed as having complexity, and this propensity for oversimplification gets reproduced in every discussion about pornography.

Raising these loathsome issues of class also offers another way of thinking about the current social preoccupation with pornography. This intensified focus on regulating and suppressing the lowest of all low things comes just as the legacy of Reaganomics has been fully realized, as gaps in U.S. income levels between high and low ends of the social spectrum have become the widest in the industrialized West, as middle-class wages are dropping, as the lower classes are expanding *and* becoming increasingly impoverished.[11] A new social compact is being negotiated by the Right, with an intensified ideology of distinctions, as those at the bottom end of the class structure (the homeless, the welfare classes, minimum-wage workers) are nonchalantly abandoned to their fates. Shifts in economic ideology require a retooled social conscience, and arguments about culture are one place these new forms of consent get negotiated—and this is the subtext of what's come to be known as the Culture Wars.[12]

Current economic realignments may seem far afield from pornography. But pornography is a space in the social imagination as well as a media form. As we'll see, interestingly, the issue of pornography is never very far away from any political argument about culture: it's been an explicit focus of these culture debates the Right has been waging over the last ten years. What do the Culture Wars stage but a duel between the canon (imagined as the high thing) and pornography (clearly, the low). Wherever arguments in favor of elite culture are made, they seem unable to resist invoking pornography (or its kissing cousin, masturbation), to represent the dangerous thing that has to be resisted. What this means, of course, is that pornography ends up being spoken about more and more frequently, and becomes ever more culturally indispensable.

Poor Joycelyn Elders. For those with short memories or limited attention spans for the scandals of the Clinton administration, Elders was our nation's first black female surgeon general, the one who made the political gaffe of suggesting that masturbation should be discussed in public schools. She was quickly forced to resign. You can imagine Elders thinking, So what's the big deal? The recent much-touted University of Chicago sex survey reports that 60 percent of men and 40 percent of women aged 18–59 masturbated in the last year, and as the joke goes, those who didn't are dirty liars.

It was the conjunction of masturbation and *education* that was the thorn in the nation's side, with the Elders imbroglio getting taken up as ammunition in the Right's attempt to re-establish what it likes to refer to as "values" in education. This is to counter what it regards as the hegemony of relativism and multiculturalism imposed by liberals intent on bringing down Western culture. Nobody bothers to say exactly what's so bad about masturbation, but the connection between it and education seems, oddly, to keep recurring in conservative arguments about culture. For example, when Roger Kimball, in *Tenured Radicals*, wants to damn what he terms "The New Sophistry" in higher education, what does he select as his target? A Modern Language Association panel titled "The Muse of Masturbation." Kimball is particularly rancorous about Duke professor Eve Kosofsky Sedgwick's contribution: a paper with the canonically incorrect title "Jane Austen and the Masturbating Girl."[13] And what about Allan Bloom's *The Closing of the American Mind*? This is the book that launched many of these education debates and authorized the cultural shift rightward with its misinvocations of the ancients—it too repeatedly deploys the terrible threat of masturbation as part of its quirky attack on popular culture and contemporary mores. When Bloom rails against his favorite bogeyman, rock and roll, it's with florid turns of phrase about its "hymns to the joys of onanism," which turns life into "a nonstop, commercially prepackaged masturbational fantasy."[14]

In fact, nowhere is the connection between sex, class, and the Right's assault on culture clearer than in this deeply weird book of Bloom's. No reviews I've come across, even those by its harshest critics, seemed to notice how closely this book resembles a sexual hygiene lecture, replete with luridly imagined scenarios of "a pubescent child whose body throbs with orgasmic rhythms" and "children of both sexes . . . stimulated to a sensual frenzy" by the music of Mick Jagger, a "shrewd middle-class boy" playing the "possessed lower-class demon." The argument Bloom seems to be making here is that if rock and roll promotes masturbation and sexual promiscuity (and Bloom seems oddly certain that it does), then rock and roll is merely a variant on pornography, which thus provides him the necessary low opposition to the summits of culture he wishes to promulgate upon us—that is, the Greeks. (For some reason, Bloom can't seem to imagine anyone beating off to the classics.)

The dismissal of popular cultural forms as "masturbatory" has a certain tedious familiarity. It's a favorite chestnut of cultural elitists, with the guilt-by-association link between the two meant to prove, by implication, that popular culture too is mindless and self-indulgent, enjoyed mainly by adolescents, the intellectually feeble, and the lower echelons. The childhood shame of guilty self-abuse is strategically annexed to confer shame onto mass culture and its audiences. And who's really so immune from this kind of shaming? Informed by self-assured intellectuals from right-wing think tanks, who read Plato in the original Greek, that your favorite leisure activity (the boob tube, usually) is similar to that embarrassing thing you don't really want to be caught doing (sinful self-pleasure), how many shame-free middlebrows are likely to respond with the prowanking line?

So masturbation is both an adolescent pastime, but at the same time has to be cordoned off from adolescents, as the outrage over Elders' remark, or Bloom's remonstrations about rock and roll, seem to indicate. The profound sense of boundaries violated evoked in these collisions of culture and masturbation indicate that these are, at root, zoning issues. And cultural zoning issues aren't so unlike other zoning issues; for example, not so unlike the referendum recently under consideration by the New York City Council, which proposed to zone where pornography can and cannot operate. Rather than attempt to eliminate porn businesses, New York instead wants to take, as one representative puts it, the "maximum degree of control" over how and where they do their business. The new restrictions would prevent sex-related businesses from operating within five hundred feet of residences, schools, or houses of worship, or within five hundred feet of one another; it would restrict their spheres of operation to parts of Times Square and push the remaining businesses into isolated manufacturing areas on the fringes of the outer boroughs. (However, the city won't force any porn shop to move until it's recouped its initial investment, in an interesting concession that after all, business is business.[15])

This municipal attempt to enforce a spatial separation between pornography and the citizenry is a bit peculiar. Who exactly are pornography's customers, if not the citizenry? Squeezing it from the center (midtown) to the periphery (the outer boroughs) and designating the home-school-church nexus as a pornography-free zone, is, like firing Elders, or like various other boundary issues that erupt periodically within local, cultural, and national landscapes, more symbolic than practical.

What appears to be at stake in these zoning debates—both the symbolic and the municipal—is the question of pornography's place within the culture: where to situate a thing that's simultaneously entirely central and entirely marginal. This gets played out in a series of cultural quagmires: how to reconcile pornography's First Amendment protection as a form of speech with the necessity to regulate its spheres of operation because its speech is transgressive? How to safeguard its vast success as free enterprise and simultaneously cordon it off from this imaginary nonmasturbating citizenry (for their own protection). The sudden national emergency Elders' comment precipitated around the need to barrier off masturbation and education from each other is a case in point, given the very conceptual incoherence of the project: cordoning children off from masturbation because masturbation is an excessively adolescent pursuit, which as everyone knows, adolescents hardly need schooling in. A high degree of magical thinking appears to permeate, and indeed, engender, these boundary issues.

Why *do* these motifs of masturbation and pornography make such frequent and highly publicized appearances in conservative arguments about culture? Summoned over and over as the thing good culture has to dedicate itself to repelling, for the purpose of staging a symbolic and ritualistic public cleansing, pornography and masturbation are then expelled once more to the periphery (the outer boroughs of culture), just to be dragged back in again to do their civic duty. Pornography seems to live on perpetual standby to represent the nadir of culture, on call to provide the necessary opposition to culture's apex, which is, of course, the canon. It's indicative of just how much the canon needs pornography as the thing to mark its own elevation against, just as much as education needs to repel masturbation—that embarrassing thing that doesn't need teaching.

These tenuous distinctions are as problematic to uphold as they are necessary to restage, and Allan Bloom's *The Closing of the American Mind,* with its rather salacious masturbation and youthful sex scenarios, is a case in point. The more time you spend discussing these dirty deeds, reluctantly invoking them, agonizing about them, expelling them, the more central, and *vivid,* pornography or masturbation become.[16] The more, like Bloom, your enterprise rubs up against the thing it's so dedicated to repelling. Bloom's slightly hysterical argument about pop culture is that it sexually manipulates the young, barbarically appealing to their unformed sexual desires, cultivating "the taste for the orgiastic states of feeling connected to sex." Popular culture is emptied of any meaning other than an inducement to masturbatory pleasure, and the popular audience is transfigured into a nation of children with a penchant for mindless self-indulgence, which Bloom waves around as if it were sticky sheets, the symptom of a moral failure. This combination of paternalism, guilt-trips, and inducements to moral reform follows the Victorian antimasturbation tract precisely, along with all its creepy obsessiveness and projection of perversity onto children. Clearly the distinction between the child who must be protected from sex and the sexualized child becomes somewhat lost here, another tenuous distinction unraveled. (And not for nothing is our favored cliché of the moral reformer the one that reveals him as just another disgusting lecher, as in Somerset Maugham's "Rain"—his missionary's obsession with thwarting sin a reaction-formation to barely contained sinful impulses.)

The Victorians invented the erotic child, and along with it a series of bizarre and sadistic contraptions like armored belts, toothed penile rings, and electric genital alarms to prevent childhood masturbation. The erotic child, then, is a child who must be punished, and in Bloom, as with the Victorians, the obsession with childhood masturbation goes hand in hand (so to speak) with the dedication to spanking as a socially sanctioned moral corrective.[17] Or rather, in this retrofitted version, which annexes popular culture to the masturbating child, it's "Daddy's Going to Spank You If You Watch Too Much TV." And you know you deserve it. After all, Bloom isn't standing alone in the nation's living room, belt in hand, issuing his parental rebukes. This book became the second-best-selling hardcover of 1987 and a number-one best-selling paperback. The erotics of discipline and punishment are a two-way street, dependent on the subterranean yearning for stern daddy figures who will lay down the law and administer the spanking you deserve for your dirty cultural habits. Bloom's "surprise success" as best-selling author hinges on the middlebrow public's eagerness to hoist naked buttocks into the air for the sweet sting of paternal discipline, its willingness to be shamed for its childish indulgence and lack of seriousness. (And at hardcover prices.) Buying into Bloom's argument about culture means taking up your place as a naughty child who needs discipline. How far is this from Strictly Spanking and its memorial to the childhood erotics of guilt and punishment?

Bound and Gagged

On the one hand, fun is fun, and who doesn't enjoy a good spanking from time to time? But on the other, what Bloom's rather melodramatic subtitle (*How Higher Education Has Failed Democracy and Impoverished the Souls of Today's Students*) makes clear about the current political context is that there's a massive renegotiation of our national sense of political possibilities under way. Democracy is no longer an entitlement of citizenship; rather, democracy accrues to those who adhere to proper participation in culture. The subtext of these national culture debates is an argument about the sustainability of the democratic project: Who deserves democracy and who doesn't? In Bloom's revisionism, democracy is failed when higher education doesn't properly educate elites to take up their places in a properly plutocratic society. The mark of that failure is that their education doesn't properly inoculate them against the taint of popular culture, which in Bloom's narrative also leaves them vulnerable to masturbation and sexual promiscuity. Or it's all sort of interchangeable. What Bloom wants from culture is that it offer training not only in more heightened forms of repression, since Bloom's version of educated citizenship depends on repudiating bodily pleasure, but that it also enforces the proper segregation between vertically imagined cultural spheres: no mixing between cultural classes—that is, no fucking down.

Bloom's horror of the body, of pleasure occurring below the neck—unless it has the requisite seriousness—is indistinguishable from his horror of democracy; that is, horror of the desires, the aspirations, the necessities of nonelites. A horror of the masturbator who is coded as body, against the philosophy-reading cognitive nobility. This book is as impassioned in its denunciation of fulfilled desire as it is celebratory of sexuality that's guilty and forbidden, difficult and angst ridden, because that's a "higher" form of sex. It's fervently nostalgic for pre–sexual liberation (and pre–gay liberation) sexuality—as nostalgic as it is for pre–counter culture, pre-sixties obedience to authority. But the main thrust of this argument is to warn elites that their cultural habits have made them indistinct from the unenlightened masses, that undeflected desire puts you into cultural decline.

Bloom, who was gay, and closeted throughout his career as a public intellectual, may have felt this to be particularly true, and was particularly well placed to make an argument that is, in effect, a coded yet eloquent plea for the merits of the closet. In this book, sublimated desire is the admission price into the elite. But the kind of middlebrow self-loathing and guilt that Bloom's book appeals to—that anxious desire to join the "top clubs"—ironically parodies the gay self-loathing of the book's obligatory homages to marriage and normative heterosexuality, and its bitter harangues against "relativism" of any kind. Not the least of which is the fact that the "cultural standards" this book strives to install might very well jeopardize the position of an openly gay college professor as any sort of cultural standard bearer for the very audiences who most adored this book, from the *National Review* crowd on down. Allan Bloom was a paid-up member of the gang—he even contributed to right-wing virulently antigay student newspapers.[18] Bloom's entitled to his contradictions, as are we all, but even though he makes a persuasive plea for the erotics of guilty sex, one might want to question the book's endless projections of perversity onto the student population at large, or question Bloom's complaints about their meaningless relationships, their superficiality, their refusal to say they love each other in bed (how does he know this? one wants to ask), in that these rebukes are so reminiscent of the kinds of stereotypes batted around about gay men during those long-gone, pre-AIDS disco days.[19]

In Bloom's argument, one in which the unredeemed masturbator falls out of democracy, while the reformed masturbator earns a chance to reenter the fold, the masturbator is, in fact, simply the popular-culture audience. That is, it's the American citizen, transformed into the figure of the naughty child and entreated to take up a position in a reform narrative. The reinvention of middlebrow culture as a venue for disseminating new grounds for finer distinctions and exclusions among the citizenry, and for the production of new forms of shame and shaming, is certainly timely given the socioeconomic transitions currently under way. New grounds for elitist rebukes of the desperate classes will come in handy. They deserve it, right? For their failings, they—these laggards, these masturbators—are jettisoned from the job market, from the welfare system, from even a place to live, and we—those with jobs, homes, family values—don't even have to feel bad about it, or wonder about the larger system that produces such harsh inequities. It's the individual. That's the usefulness of distinction-making in a context of declining resources, and why it's useful to pay attention to how pornography gets wielded as a political metaphor for the low thing, precisely when the low thing becomes a crucial political space.

What also motor Bloom's impassioned argument against embodied desire and its fulfillment are the meanings and subtexts that might accrue from those experiences, and you can tell that from his malevolence toward the sixties. The sixties are this book's bad object. Bloom is still railing, anachronistically, about the bad manners of campus protesters and fulminating against the black-power movement, but his greatest antipathy is for sixties-style sexual politics. But the sixties weren't *only* about having a lot of sex: the premise of sixties sexual liberation was that sex offers a window onto other political and social forms of gratification—even onto utopian idealism, and reimagined futures. The experience of gratification, even cheap, solo, or "unserious" gratification, we learned from the sixties, has political resonance: it can migrate and reverberate into other social spheres. A movie like *Coming Home* (1978) could only have been made post-sixties: during the height of the war in Viet Nam, Jane Fonda has terrible sex with her militaristic-creep husband, Bruce Dern, then her first orgasm with paraplegic antiwar vet Jon Voight. Good sex is put into analogy with antiwar activism, bad sex with Nixon's secret war and the official lies of his administration. The connection between sexual repression and authoritarian political styles was a fundamental premise of sixties counterculture (borrowing from the Frankfurt School and, particularly, Herbert Marcuse's work), and it's a connection Allan Bloom's best-seller, relying on our cultural and political amnesia, dedicated itself to reinstating.

Popular culture, including pornography, and however much both the Left and Right disdain to admit it, is like masturbation, a fundamental access to gratification for its participants. Psychoanalysis, which takes masturbation, as it does most other seemingly mundane things, seriously, sees in it the reproduction of the experience of an original satisfaction of desire, like thirst or hunger. What masturbation implies then, thematically, is the simple possibility of a need met. Given the way needs issues open onto larger questions like social resources, distribution, entitlements, and even the organization of work, what gratification means politically is a question worth thinking seriously about, particularly in the absence of any official political discourse that seriously entertains the question. It's telling that even the most elemental, bare-boned expression of gratification —masturbation (a distinctly fleeting, solitary, and nascent form of gratification)—should have become a national political issue in the first place, and when it did, have been so strikingly, so endlessly surrounded by embarrassment and shame, by an elaborate web of prohibitions, stigma, and eternal nervous jokes. What's clear is that shame is produced in forms available for political mobilization, to be annexed to whatever minute and mundane spheres of freedom embodied subjects can create for themselves: whether masturbation, or the pleasures of popular culture, as stupid and commodified as they are, or the almost forgotten utopian aspirations of the sixties. Shame is particularly available for mobilization now, it seems, if the Elders case is any indication. And that's one reason that feminist attacks on pornography are so depressing and so politically problematic, particularly to the extent that feminism envisions itself as a movement dedicated to expanding human freedom and possibility in the sphere of gender.

When *Time's* "People" column announced the engagement of feminist antipornography crusader Catharine MacKinnon and antipsychoanalytic Lothario, Jeffrey Masson, raised eyebrows and suppressed smirks reigned. MacKinnon has made the case, in a series of powerful polemics, that sex with men is largely indistinguishable from rape (which is not prohibited, but merely regulated in this country, she says); rape and pornography are at the heart of heterosexuality, and women have no ability to freely consent to sex even when they think they do, given the coerciveness of male sexuality, whose apex is the pornography industry. She's also prone to issuing stern directives like "If your sexuality is pornographic, then you're not entitled to your sexuality." A University of Michigan law professor, MacKinnon is the coauthor, with the even more polemical Andrea Dworkin ("The hatred of women is a source of sexual pleasure for men in its own right. Intercourse appears to be the expression of that contempt in its pure form. . . ."[20]), of antipornography legislation that defines pornography as "the graphic, sexually explicit subordination of women whether in pictures or words" and as a violation of women's civil rights, which would allow us to sue pornographers for civil damages if we suffer due to their products. (According to MacKinnon and Dworkin, to be a woman is, by definition, to suffer harm from pornography. All women do.) The advantage of this form of legislation is that it would, presumably, hinder the ability of the porn industry to do business, while not technically being censorship, which we still have something of an aversion to in this country. Various municipalities have attempted to enact the MacKinnon-Dworkin legislation, without success thus far. There's that small matter of freedom of speech, that Bill of Rights thing. However, a version of this ordinance has been enacted in Canada under what's known as the *Butler* decision. As the ACLU's Nadine Strossen points out, the effect has primarily been to increase the government's ability to harass gay, lesbian, and feminist bookstores: half of all feminist bookstores in Canada had material seized at customs in the first two and a half years following the ruling. Feminist and lesbian books and magazines have been ruled by Canadian judges to "harm women" under *Butler*. Two of Andrea Dworkin's own books were seized at the border, lest their sexual explicitness incite those impressionable Canadians to unspeakable acts.[21] Ignoring this shoddy treatment of her pal, MacKinnon soldiers on in her quest to enact similar legislation here.

The flamboyant Jeffrey Masson, on the other hand, is probably most famous for having injudiciously divulged to *New Yorker* writer Janet Malcolm that he'd had his way with over a thousand women, and then suing her for fabricating quotes, although the thousand-women figure wasn't one of the quotes he disputed—leading *Spy* magazine to refer to MacKinnon on more than one occasion as Masson's thousand-and-first lover. But what's most interesting about the MacKinnon-Masson coupledom is the way it demonstrates the essential connection between the antipornography movement and the antipsychoanalysis movement, with Masson serving as a bombastic fulcrum point between the two. If psychoanalysis is the thing that comes closest to demystifying pornography, then a charismatic antipsychoanalytic guru is just what the antipornography movement most requires, particularly one who cuts such a wide swath through the media. Given that psychoanalytic theory is largely devoted to explicating the complexities of fantasy in the individual, the questions Masson's work raises—and those it fails to raise—are an opportunity to explore these links between antipsychoanalytic and antipornographic credos, specifically on the fundamental issues of fantasy and identification.

By this point we've all come to know quite a bit more about Jeffrey Masson's inner life than is perhaps strictly good for us, as Masson is a man (not unlike Larry Flynt) dedicated to acting out elaborate psychodramas upon the national stage on a fairly regular basis. These mostly have to do with his intense sense of injury: injustice awaits him at every turn. He's a man for whom scores are never settled: his métier is the extended grudge match, his favorite recreation the multi-million-dollar lawsuit, and his preferred sportswear the mantle of victimhood. A former Sanskrit scholar turned psychoanalyst, Masson first came to prominence when he was fired from his job as director of the Sigmund Freud Archives, after he'd somewhat abruptly and quite publicly renounced Freud and the foundations of psychoanalysis in the pages of the *New York Times*. Nonplussed that this was anything of a problem for his bosses, famed psychoanalyst Kurt Eissler, who had taken Masson under his wing and treated him as something of a surrogate son (and whom Masson named in his lawsuit), and for Anna Freud, who had allowed him access to her home and to the entirety of her father's papers (a privilege denied the rest of the world's scholars given that most of the archive is under seal until sometime in the next century), he sued for $13 million, charging that his freedom of speech had been violated. The analytic community charged that he had failed to understand the intellectual foundations of psychoanalysis.

The contretemps between Masson and psychoanalysis was recounted by Janet Malcolm in a series of *New Yorker* articles.[22] Masson then sued Malcolm for $10 million, monomaniacally stalking her for eleven years through the courtrooms of the nation in a libel suit that was thrown out of court twice—including by the U.S. Court of Appeals—and that he pursued all the way to the Supreme Court, which reinstated it. A first trial found for Masson but the jury deadlocked on damages. A second trial found in Janet Malcolm's favor on three of the five disputed quotes. Masson is now apparently pursuing plans for a third trial.[23]

In addition to his victimhood at the hands of Eissler and Malcolm, Masson has done public battle with his former Toronto psychoanalyst, whom he charges with being abusive and late to sessions; he's accused his parents of sexual abuse, along with a family maid who he says fondled him when he was eight—although he says he enjoyed it at the time; and threatened to ruin the career of a reviewer who wrote a nasty review of MacKinnon's last book. These are just the highlights. His intellectual work too is peopled by victims: a series of books on the crimes of psychiatry, a memoir about his family's and his own maltreatment at the hands of a self-styled guru, an article on the connection between pornography and the "pro-incest lobby," and most recently, a coauthored book on the emotional scars of animals.

This thematic repetition compulsion lends a certain murkiness to Masson's scholarship. He writes about pornography and psychoanalysis as if they were, in all important respects, indistinguishable from each other: both machines for the production of victims. And both fundamentally devoted to promoting incest: pornography directly, and psychoanalysis by suppressing evidence of it. Of course the contributing roles of either fantasy or childhood sexuality in either scene is summarily ruled out, which means that his argument with psychoanalysis and his analysis of pornography have exactly the same structure: an innocent presexual world of children (or women) is fouled and corrupted by the introduction of sexuality by perverse adults (or men). His antiporn and antipsychoanalysis positions give him all sorts of credentials with feminists who don't seem to notice the implicit analogy of women with children. Having retooled his war with Freud into an antipornography crusade, MacKinnon and Masson are now the antipornography movement's preeminent power couple: the Bob and Liz Dole of victim feminism. (Although Andrea Dworkin's longtime boyfriend John Stoltenberg has recently come out with his own antiporn manifesto, so there's competition on that front.)

Masson's problem with psychoanalysis concerns the issue known as Freud's renunciation of his "seduction theory." This was an early hypothesis of Freud's (held for two years from 1895 to 1897) that traced the origins of neurotic symptoms and particularly hysteria—rife in turn-of-the-century Vienna—to childhood sexual abuse or early sexual trauma. The theory derived from the fact that very nearly all of these early psychoanalytic patients reported such incidents in the course of treatment. However, Freud soon revised seduction theory, shifting his focus from real sexual trauma to the fantasies that such experiences could, would, or had happened. In other words, toward the theory that the Oedipal narrative—libidinal desire for the parent—is a universal experience. The Oedipus complex is a theory about how children navigate their way toward adult sexuality (and especially for women, toward heterosexuality from an early bisexuality) through the successful resolution and internalization of these Oedipal desires; unsuccessful resolution was "the nucleus of neurosis."

This turn in Freud's thinking resulted in most of the important foundations of psychoanalytical thought: the theory of childhood sexuality, and an emphasis on the importance of psychical over practical reality. Freud didn't deny the reality of "seduction" actually experienced by children, but he did come to realize that it was impossible to tell the difference between a real memory and a fantasy cathected or charged with affect. But for psychoanalysis, there isn't a simple opposition between reality and fantasy. Fantasy isn't equated with illusion: rather, "psychic reality" is construed as a third term. It has *reality* for the individual. In addition, the fantasy and the reality of seduction aren't completely unrelated, as children experience sexual feelings in, say, the course of ordinary hygiene maneuvers parents may perform—baths or toilet training. (In fact, Masson's own charges of sexual abuse against his parents center around just these kinds of hygiene seductions.[24] And it seems fairly likely that this kind of early erotic experience factors into the pornography of infantilism, like *Diapers*.) This insistence on the importance of psychic reality, and on the unconscious and its role in neurosis, is precisely what distinguishes psychoanalysis from other psychological theories and therapies.[25]

Masson's position, asserted in his book *The Assault on Truth,* is that Freud was wrong and *knew* he was wrong—consciously or unconsciously—in renouncing the seduction theory, and this "failure of courage" undermines the entire foundation of psychoanalytic thought. The scale of Masson's revisionist ambition is evident in a remark of his that Malcolm quotes, to the effect that when his own view of seduction theory took hold, "they'd have to recall every patient since 1901. It would be like the Pinto." Specifically Masson thinks Freud lied (or suppressed the truth) about the actual incidence of incest and child sexual abuse in society in order to ingratiate himself with the Viennese bourgeoisie and solidify his own position of respectability, and that this sort of lying permeates the entire profession of psychoanalysis to this day.[26]

There's no doubt that psychoanalytic theory has been abused in clinical situations by a male-dominated psychiatric establishment, and primarily to women's detriment: in the wrong hands, psychoanalysis is just another opportunity for the exercise of male domination. (And in some cases, the wrong hands were Freud's, notably in the infamous Dora case.) It's also clear that Freud himself wasn't always capable of the sort of "psychoanalytic listening" that refuses to invoke external realities to counter an analysand's fantasies. But of course, psychoanalysis isn't alone in providing opportunities for male domination, which is abundant in every other social institution you can think of— marriage, education, work, sex, the law, ad infinitum—but along the way it's produced important cultural and psychological insights. The argument rages over whether it "describes" or "prescribes" patriarchal norms, but nevertheless, it's been frequently employed by feminists to help fathom the social construction of gender and sexuality, and to interrogate the kinds of issues Masson and MacKinnon refuse to regarding pornography and sexuality.

Masson's main official contribution to the pornography debates is an essay in the collection *Men Confront Pornography* arguing that incest pornography is the very nucleus of pornography—its prototypical form—produced and distributed by the "proincest lobby," as he puts it. (I confess I haven't heard of this group. Whom do they lobby exactly—Congress?) In the same way that MacKinnon's work relies on a slippage between pornography and violence, which become indistinguishable from each other when she's through with them, Masson yokes all of pornography to this one subgenre (which consists entirely of paperback fiction), concluding that all pornography is fundamentally devoted to promoting incest.

What he argues is that there's a contradiction at the heart of the incest-porn genre, because these books claim to address readers who merely enjoy the *fantasy* of incest, yet the rhetorical mode of many of the books is to present themselves in the form of real case histories. But their narrative voices are unlike "real" accounts of incest by "survivors." In fact, there's nothing "real" in these books, he says. The books may be fantasy, but because incest itself is not fantasy, incest pornography is really "a form of action" that serves to justify incest. (The line that pornography is a form of action, not a form of speech, is MacKinnon's premise in *Only Words*.[27])

This argument may be difficult to follow, but its larger purpose is clear: to annihilate the position that pornography is or can ever be a fantasy medium. Masson finally even comes out and says that he sees the term "fantasy" as merely a synonym for "lies." Therefore, of course, an incest fantasy simply can't exist—it would be either the precursor to an action, an excuse, or a memory. Masson also claims to know (although he doesn't explain how) that male readers *don't* read these as fantasies, that ordinary readers *can't* read them and not be harmed by them, and that child molesters read them as evidence that they've done nothing wrong, because they believe that these case histories—which often portray girls who either enjoy incest or are the instigators of it—are genuine. He informs us that the public at large believes that incest is harmless and a natural act, a belief enforced by these books. It's clear that Masson's argument with pornography is the same argument he's having with Freud, who in this account becomes the original incest pornographer, having reduced real cases of incest to "the overheated fantasies of adolescent girls."[28]

Now one might want to read Masson's argument that fantasy doesn't exist as a strategic political argument against those within psychoanalysis and in the culture generally who have perhaps thought that incest can't exist. Incest does exist. But the stakes in this argument are whether there's such a thing as an Oedipal fantasy, and by extension, any other kind of fantasy: Masson won't entertain the idea that there can be both Oedipal fantasies *and* actual incest (or that this might even be part of what screws up incest victims so much), or that acknowledging the existence of incest fantasies isn't the same thing as declaring open season for child sex. Something impedes him from recognizing the contradictions and murkiness inherent in the field of desire. (Which also leads him to insist that there are no forms of pornography whose desire is not to "subordinate and do harm to another person.") What's at stake in denying the existence of fantasy, and insisting so vehemently and so repetitively that only absolute literalness and consciousness govern the human psyche and its desires?

As Masson wages his private wars with what can only seem to the casual observer like a succession of Oedipal figures— Freud, Eissler, his own psychoanalyst, the psychoanalytic establishment, his father, his father's guru—all of whom are knocked off their paternal perches one by one while Masson plays the aggrieved victim, as he finds within pornography another opportunity to continue this battle, all the while beating his fists against the concept of psychical reality and the very existence of the unconscious (concepts that might just shed some light on this interesting cast of characters), the question that psychoanalytic theory would pose is that of *identification*. Where exactly is the subject (the fantasizer) within the fantasy?

Psychoanalytic theory proposes that in fantasy (and I'm adding, in fantasy genres like pornography), identification is mobile, unpredictable, and not bound by either one's actual gender or by practical reality. *Fantasies don't in any literal way represent desires*: they're the setting for desires. What looks straightforward, like, say, a victim fantasy or a rape fantasy, isn't.

A rape fantasy doesn't represent a desire to be raped. Oedipal fantasies mask their desires behind any number of subterfuges. What and where is the real desire? It's coded within the fantasy, and has to be interpreted. Your identification can be with any aspect of the fantasy, and this isn't necessarily conscious: in the classic "a father is beating a child" and as we saw in the DePew case, identification can be with the father, the child, the implement, a bystander observing the beating, or with *any* aspect of the scene that engages your affect. Identification doesn't mean you like it or want to do it. It may be ambivalent, or based on relics and repressions from the past. All that it means is that something hooks you about the scene, and you don't necessarily know what.

It's crucial to note, in thinking through the identification question in pornography, that identification takes place *across gender lines*: as a male you can identify with a female character and vice versa. This is completely obvious in movies, which are a form of popular fantasy: women audience members identify with male protagonists, men with women. Not always, but often enough. Film theorist Carol Clover has made an analogous argument about male viewers of horror films, contending that it's a more victim-identified genre than generally acknowledged. Horror gives male audiences the opportunity to identify with the fear and pain of female heroines (who are often both heroes and victims), because different character functions (the victim, the hero) resonate with competing parts of the viewer's psyche. Genres like horror are an opportunity to reenact basic residual conflicts, given the way they engage such a range of repressed fears and desires. What Clover argues against, and my argument about pornography reiterates, is the simplistic presumption that *all* male viewing experiences of horror films, or pornography, are at root sadistic—that is, singularly identified with whatever power, domination, or cruelty is operating within the scene.[29]

The complexity of identification is an issue that neither MacKinnon or Masson are willing to address in their work. This same failure of complexity also permeated the case of *United States v. DePew*: it's a failure upon which the entire case was predicated. *DePew* also reveals quite vividly that these aren't merely intellectual arguments or abstract issues—they filter through the social structure and impress themselves on public policy, on methods of policing the citizenry, on judges and juries. Insisting that one's own identifications are universal—as do MacKinnon and Masson—both misunderstands the complexity of the issue and has consequences in the world. *None* of us comes to these issues absent a biography, or absent psychic complexity. (Which is probably why much has been made of the fact that MacKinnon's own father was a Republican U.S. Court of Appeals judge who wrote a decision declaring sexual expression in the workplace as a "normal and expectable social pattern" and that MacKinnon's early career was devoted to workplace sexual harassment issues.) Refusing to acknowledge the complexity of either one's own or anyone else's identifications can be, in cases like Dan DePew's, tragic.

But it's Jeffrey Masson himself who inadvertently demonstrates that the nature of identification in fantasy is shifting *and* nongendered, when as a pornography viewer his identification is clearly with the *female* characters, and with whom, as his article on incest porn demonstrates, he imaginatively identifies. Maybe their victimization echoes what he sees as his own; maybe he takes umbrage on their behalf because they're unfairly portrayed as conscienceless seducers. Who knows? The point is that identification within the pornographic scenario is completely unpredictable, and not gender bound. And if Jeffrey Masson has the capacity to identify across gender lines, and finds in pornography's themes and narratives a psychic home to furnish with his own imaginative identifications, why isn't this just as true for every other pornography viewer, whose psyches are just as complicated, and whose identifications just as variant?

Arguments about Catharine MacKinnon's work have usually centered either on the violence her positions do to the First Amendment or on the fact that many women actually like pornography as opposed to feeling victimized by it. (MacKinnon habitually refers to her critics as dupes of the "pornography lobby.") One of the most systematic recent critiques is ACLU president Nadine Strossen's *Defending Pornography*, which lays out the MacKinnon-Dworkin position in detail and mounts trenchant arguments against it.[30] My only argument with Strossen is that she treats what she calls "MacDworkinism" as a fundamentally coherent, rational, yet incorrect set of positions, whereas my view is that MacDworkinism is fundamentally irrational, but at the same time, correct. In other words, its truths are in the realm of psychical reality. Pornography *does,* in an emotional sense, do profound violence—emotional violence—to some women. However, for women who hate pornography, the violence it inflicts is to female identity and "female sensibility," which perhaps explains something about why so many women are drawn to MacDworkinism: it expresses the real outrage and injury we may feel, without bothering to delve too deeply into its preconditions.

Not all women dislike pornography; some even like it a lot. So obviously there's a spectrum of female identities. But the problem most women have who don't like porn is that they don't recognize the female characters in it as "like me"—either physically, or in their desires. These big-breasted porno bimbos want to have sex all the time, with any guy no matter how disgusting, will do *anything,* moan like they like it, and aren't repulsed by male body fluids—in fact, adore them—wherever they land.[31] Women who dislike porn refer to this as a male fantasy, but what exactly is it a fantasy about? Well, it seems like a fantasy of a one-gender world,[32] a world in which male and female sexuality is completely commensurable, as opposed to whatever sexual incompatibilities actually exist.

Heterosexual pornography creates a fantastical world composed of two sexes but one gender, and that one gender looks a lot more like what we think of (perhaps stereotypically) as "male." Pornography's premise is this: What would a world in which men and women were sexually alike look like? (The romance industry proposes a similar hypothesis in reverse: What would the world look like if men were emotionally and romantically compatible with women?) So pornography's fantasy is also of gender malleability, although one in which it's women who should be the malleable ones. Whereas feminism's (and romance fiction's) paradigm of gender malleability is mostly that men should change. It's possible that the women who are most offended by pornography are those most invested in the idea of femininity as something static and stable, as something inborn that inheres within us. ("Women are like this, men are like that.") But of course, sexuality *is* completely malleable (and sexuality is a component of gender, by which I mean masculinity and femininity), altering radically over history, or with education level, age, religion, etc.

One model for looking at pornography would be as a kind of science fiction; that is, as a fantasy about futurity, whose setting is the present. We don't get offended when science fiction imagines different futures, even dystopic ones set in worlds that look like our own. Of course one reason that women, and particularly feminists, have a hard time either enjoying pornography as an interesting gender fantasy, or dismissing it as a harmless gender fantasy, is our worry that in a world in which men have more social power than women, men have the power to force their fantasy of a one-gender world onto unwilling women, who have their own ideas about how female sexuality should feel. But *is* pornography proffered (and enjoyed) as a form of propaganda? And if you think so, why presume that pornography alone, among the vast range of cultural forms, works as indoctrination, whereas every other popular genre is understood as inhabiting the realm of fiction, entertainment, even ideas, *not* as having megalomaniacal ambitions to transform the world into itself? We don't spend a lot of time worrying that viewers of pro wrestling will suddenly be seized with some all-consuming impulse to wrestle innocent passersby to the ground. On what grounds are such megalomaniacal intentions imputed to pornography?

Despite whatever chagrin it may induce, offended parties (male and female) might want to reconceptualize pornography's offenses as a form of social knowledge. These offenses have eloquence. They have social meaning. Besides, what's so terrible about being offended? About having all your presuppositions and the very core of your identity shaken up? (Well, maybe a lot.) But looking at pornography wouldn't be an issue worth bothering about unless there was more at stake than sexual pleasure, which—while I hardly mean to malign sex, which has enough bricks thrown at it these days—isn't the only reason pornographic fantasy is worth fighting for.

A psychoanalytically-inflected theory of fantasy suggests the mobilities and complexities of identification and proposes that pornography viewers can imaginatively identify with any aspect of the pornographic fantasy scenario or all of them: with any character, action, detail, or even with the form or sequence of the fantasy. One key aspect of pornography's form is that there's so very very much of it, it's so vast and endless. It never runs out.

Why is there so much pornography? Why the sheer repetition? It may be that there's something inherent in human desire that defeats the capacity of anything to satisfy it. For Freud that's because any sexual object is always a poor substitute for the original one you couldn't have, with that unfulfillable wish taking the form of a succession of substitute objects. (Freud also related repetition to trauma, to the need to master psychic injury through the compulsive return to its scene of origin.) It may also be that within consumer capitalism, our desires have to be endlessly activated to keep us tied to the treadmill of the production-consumption cycle: If we ceased having unfulfillable desires and stopped trying to quell them with a succession of consumer durables and commodified pleasures, instant economic chaos would soon follow.

Or perhaps the abundance of pornography—such an inherent aspect of the genre—resonates with a primary desire for plenitude, a desire for counter-scarcity economies in any number of registers: economic, emotional, or sexual. Pornography proposes an economy of pleasure in which not only is there always enough, there's even more than you could possibly want. That has to have a certain grab to it, given the way that scarcity is the context and the buried threat of most of our existences, whatever form it takes—not enough love, sex, or money are favorite standbys.

Preserving an enclave for fantasy is an important political project for the following reason: pornography provides a forum to engage with a realm of contents and materials exiled from public view and from the dominant culture, and this may indeed encompass unacceptable, improper, transgressive contents, including, at times, staples of the unconscious like violence, misogyny, or racism. But at the same time, within this realm of transgression, there's the freedom, displaced from the social world of limits and proprieties, to indulge in a range of longings and desires without regard to the appropriateness and propriety of those desires, and without regard to social limits on resources, object choices, perversity, or on the anarchy of the imagination.

Whatever the local expressions of longings for plenitude—and perhaps longings for sex, love, and other kinds of human fulfillment aren't unrelated to more material issues like the social distribution of resources—the freedom to fantasize different futures, and different possibilities for individual, bodily, and collective fulfillment, *is* a crucial political space. Perhaps when issues of pleasure, plenitude, and freedom are articulated more frequently in places other than fantasy genres like pornography they won't need to find their expression only in these coded and pornographic forms.

I asked Daniel DePew, at one point in our conversations, what his life would have been like without S&M. I somewhat expected him to say that he couldn't imagine that possibility. Instead he launched into this detailed fantasy.

"I would be a nice nine-to-fiver, working in the electronics field, moving my way up in management, working myself to death, wanting a three-bedroom house with a dog and a thirty-year mortgage and the above-ground pool out in suburbia, with my lover," he said in one breath. "Do you mean it would be dull and conventional?" I asked. "No," he said, surprising me. "It probably would have been bliss." I asked why. "Because behind all the typicality, the sameness, the humdrum suburban life, there's *love* there. I'd have my lover, we'd go play bridge, we'd love each other, and we'd care about each other, we'd have this idyllic perfect existence. We'd wake up on Sunday morning and go to the MCC [Mormon] church, then we'd come back to the house and it's our turn to have the barbecue brunch, and everybody'd come over to our house for barbecue, and we'd just have a nice life, two men together, sharing and loving and caring."

"Did you think you could have a life like that?" I asked. "That's what I wanted," he said. "My goal was to somehow miraculously, down the road, move to Montana with my lover, buy a big old farmhouse with four rooms upstairs and four rooms downstairs, have a couple of dogs . . ." He trailed off. The bucolic charm of this life surprised and moved me—especially compared to the bleak, loveless prison world that surrounded us. But then of course it was his capacity for vivid fantasies that got him into such trouble in the first place. "So you *wanted* to give up S&M?" I asked. "Oh no, that would have been part of it," he corrected me quickly, forgetting that the original question had been what his life would have been like without S&M. It was clear that he couldn't imagine love—and this *was* a fantasy about love—without sadomasochism, which, to his eventual misfortune at the hands of the state, had been his only path to that very necessary thing.

In playing back the tapes of the interview, I realized that I kept returning to the question of why DePew felt the need to be punished. What was at the origin of that desire? I asked this question a number of times, and DePew kept explaining to me, patiently, that for him it wasn't punishment, it had to do with proving himself and proving his masculinity. Five minutes later I would ask the question again. Like his jury, I was missing the point. The components out of which we construct our sexual and emotional repertoires are completely individualistic—raw materials, so to speak. The same element will have a completely different meaning to two different people: not punishment, but triumph; not pain, but love. Daniel DePew's solution was a creative one, given the limited means available to him (and to us all): In sadomasochistic fantasy he found a solution that let him go on.

In his instructions to the jury on how they might infer DePew's intentions, Judge Ellis grudgingly admitted that there was no way of fathoming or scrutinizing the operations of the human mind. In *United States v. DePew,* no one bothered to try— Daniel DePew was too convenient a receptacle for cultural anxieties and fearsome fantasies of the bogeyman, a fall guy for adult violence to children. So we've locked him up and thrown away the key, as if that will solve our problems.

The failures of prosecutors and jury to bring either insight or empathy to the DePew case is typical of the difficulty we seem to have, as a culture, in coming to terms with the existence of pornography. The project of understanding pornography, or worse, of understanding someone else's pornographic fantasies, seems to provoke only massive failures of empathy and cold punitiveness. The rationale is always that it will "lead to something," to the harm of some innocent, usually a woman or a child (often the same thing in the cultural imagination). Perhaps it *is* our innocence that pornography harms. But nothing has such diabolic effects or causes 100 percent guaranteed harm—as pornography is said to by its opponents—but some monster from the imagination. These monsters include imaginary snuff films, and imaginary pollution threats, and pornography as an all-purpose but imaginary explanation for the real horrors of rape and domestic violence.[33]

The preceding chapters have cataloged some good reasons for this profound sense of injury at pornography's hands: pornography is transgressive and socially unsettling. It assaults the idea that genders are handed down from God and nature. Its class aspirations are downwardly mobile in a society that fears and loathes downward mobility. It's so profoundly antiaesthetic that it can even be, at times, viscerally upsetting. It dredges up long-repressed materials that we're much happier relegating to the trash heap of the unconscious. And it's far safer, and more gratifying to imagine its audience—especially if you count yourself as not among its members—as scuzzy, pustule-ridden perverts than as your friends, spouse, or clergyman.

But if pornographic fantasy was, for one man, a circuitous path to love (and to some degree, I believe, to repair, as well), if the materials that constitute pornography are this close to the fundamentals of selfhood, then pornography manages to penetrate to the marrow of who we are as a culture and as psyches. What better than pornography understands that amalgam of complexes, repressions, and identifications we call "me"? It may strike too close for comfort, but developing some kind of rapprochement with it is the only politic solution: pornography's not going away anytime soon. (Sorry, neither is the business of mass culture, or its commodified pleasures.) In the meantime, maybe we can learn a few things from its civil disobedience.

Notes

Preface

1. See *The Invention of Pornography: Obscenity and the Origins of Modernity, 1500–1800*, ed. Lyn Hunt (New York: Zone, 1993).

2. Linda Williams' pivotal book on pornography, *Hard Core: Power, Pleasure, and the "Frenzy of the Visible"* (Berkeley: University of California Press, 1989) evades the proporn/antiporn dilemma, and although my argument departs from Williams' in many respects, her work has influenced me significantly. Angela Carter's *The Sadeian Woman and the Ideology of Pornography* (New York: Pantheon, 1978) has also been important in shaping my thinking.

　　For essays in the "pro-sex" tradition, along with a variety of other feminist anticensorship approaches to porn, see *Caught Looking: feminism, pornography & censorship*, ed. Kate Ellis et al. (New York: Caught Looking, 1986); *Powers of Desire: The Poli-*

tics of Sexuality, ed. Ann Snitow et al. (New York: Monthly
Review Press, 1983), especially Ellen Willis, "Feminism, Mor-
alism and Pornography," 460–67; and *Pleasure and Danger:
Exploring Female Sexuality*, ed. Carole S. Vance (Boston:
Routledge & Kegan Paul, 1984), especially Gayle Rubin, "Thinking Sex: Notes for a Radical Theory of the Politics of Sexuality," 267–319.

3. See *Good Girls/Bad Girls: Feminists and Sex Trade Workers
Face to Face*, ed. Laurie Bell (Toronto: Seal Press, 1987); also
Anne McClintock, "Sex Workers and Sex Work," *Social Text* 37
(Winter 1993): 1–10. See also "World Charter for Prostitutes'
Rights" in the same issue.

4. Lauren Berlant's work on citizenship, fantasy, and national
culture provides an important model in suggesting ways to read
the political aspirations and the *optimism* inherent in cultural
forms like these. Her work inspires this one in many ways. See
*The Queen of America Goes to Washington City: Essays on Sex and
Citizenship* (Durham, N.C.: Duke University Press, forthcoming).

5. By "us" or "we" I mean dominant culture, within which different individuals obviously have varying reactions, and alongside which there are disparate subcultural sensibilities as well.
What I mean by dominant culture in this context is the sensibility that pornography means to unsettle.

Chapter One

1. I've reconstructed the narrative of the case based on interviews
with Daniel DePew and with his attorney, James Lowe, also
through trial transcripts, FBI transcripts of wiretapped phone conversations, computer messages, and bugged meetings, police logs

on the unfolding investigation, arrest and parole reports, and newspaper articles. I also had phone conversations with Officer Rodrigues ("Bobby") and Dean Lambey's attorney, William Linka.

2. David van Biema, "Robbing the Innocents," *Time* (December 27, 1993): 31.

3. Although there have been over twelve thousand accusations of Satanic ritual abuse over the last decade—including highly publicized cases like the McMartin preschool case in LA—not one case has been substantiated, though many lives have been ruined in the process. One example is Margaret Kelly Michaels, at the time of her arrest a twenty-two-year-old aspiring actress working part-time as a day-care teacher, who was finally released after spending five years in prison when her conviction on charges of multiple child sexual abuse was overturned because the trial was riddled with "egregious prosecutorial abuses." Daniel Goleman, "Proof Lacking for Ritual Abuse by Satanists," *New York Times* (October 31, 1994), and Evelyn Nieves, "New Jersey Sex Abuse Case Ends with Charges Dropped," *New York Times* (December 3, 1994).

4. As has been widely reported, the U.S. now has the second highest imprisonment rate in the world, surpassing that of South Africa, and exceeded only by Russia.

5. Nadine Strossen quotes a figure of 3 to 8 percent in *Defending Pornography* (New York: Scribner's, 1995): 143.

6. Fred Strebeigh, "Defining Law on the Feminist Frontier," *New York Times Magazine* (October 6, 1991): 29. MacKinnon also discusses snuff films in *Only Words* (Cambridge, Mass.: Harvard University Press, 1993): 15–18 and 23–26.

7. "Morgenthau Finds Film Dismembering Was Indeed a Hoax," *New York Times* (March 10, 1976). A detailed account of the controversy surrounding the film can be found in Eithne Johnson and Eric Schaefer, "Soft Core/Hard Gore: *Snuff* as a Crisis in Meaning," *Journal of Film and Video* (Summer–Fall 1993): 40–59.

8. Catherine Bennett, "A Prophet and Porn," *The Guardian* (May 27, 1994): T20.

9. Sigmund Freud, "A Child Is Being Beaten: A Contribution to the Origin of Sexual Perversions," in *Sexuality and the Psychology of Love* (New York: MacMillan, 1963): 107–32.

Chapter Two

1. Susan Gubar, "Representing Pornography: Feminism, Criticism, and Depictions of Female Violation," in *For Adult Users Only*, ed. Susan Gubar and Joan Huff (Bloomington: Indiana University Press, 1989): 48.

2. Louise Kaplan, *Female Perversions* (New York: Doubleday, 1991): 246–49. Also Robert J. Stoller, M.D., "Transvestism in Women," in his *Observing the Erotic Imagination* (New Haven, Conn.; Yale University Press, 1985): 135–56.

3. No vice cop or state's attorney official that I spoke to would confirm that transvestite material is particularly targeted, but numerous porn-store managers assured me that this is the case—although some risk carrying some transvestite material. It was impossible to get any law enforcement official to openly discuss pornography regulation, but it's clear that various forms of por-

nography are targeted, if only because those are the categories that are locally unavailable. Lactating women is one such category. Bestiality is another—this means you can freely slaughter and eat animals, but you just can't have sex with them, which is surely not any *less* humane.

4. Kaplan, 23; Stoller, 136.

5. Barbara Rose, "Self-Portraiture: Theme with a Thousand Faces," *Art in America* (January/February 1975): 66–73.

6. The "aura" reference is to Walter Benjamin's well-known essay "The Work of Art in the Age of Mechanical Reproduction," in *Illuminations* (New York: Schocken, 1969): 217–51.

7. Arthur Danto, "Photography and Performance: Cindy Sherman's Stills," in Cindy Sherman, *Untitled Film Stills/Cindy Sherman* (New York: Rizzoli, 1990): 5–14.

8. Kaplan, 9.

9. See Joan Riviere, "Womanliness as a Masquerade," in *Formations of Fantasy*, ed. Cora Kaplan (New York: Methuen, 1986): 35–44, for another view of female impersonation by women.

10. Stoller, 49.

11. P. Gay, *Art and Act: On Causes in History—Manet, Gropius, Mondrian* (New York: Harper & Row, 1976): 225–26. Quoted by Francis V. O'Connor, "The Psychodynamics of the Frontal Self-Portrait," in *Psychoanalytic Perspectives on Art*, ed. Mary Mathews Gedo (Hillsdale, New Jersey: Analytic Press, 1985): 197.

12. J. Laplanche and J.-B. Pontalis, *The Language of Psychoanalysis* (New York: Norton, 1973): 432.

13. Stoller, 44–69.

14. See also Janine Chasseguet-Smirgel, *Creativity and Perversion* (New York: Norton, 1984): 89.

15. Pierre Bourdieu, *Distinction: A Social Critique of the Judgment of Taste* (Cambridge, Mass.: Harvard University Press, 1984): 54.

16. O'Connor, 198.

17. Peter Bürger, *Theory of the Avant-Garde* (Minneapolis: University of Minnesota Press, 1984).

18. For a feminist analysis of transvestism see Annie Woodhouse, *Fantastic Women: Sex, Gender and Transvestism* (New Brunswick, N.J.: Rutgers University Press, 1989), which, as the author says, "is not a study which is particularly sympathetic to transvestism" (xiii). See also Marjorie Garber, *Vested Interests: Cross-Dressing and Cultural Anxiety* (New York: Routledge, 1992), which although primarily concerned with the figure of the transvestite across Western culture, also regards the gender and sexual politics of transvestism from a feminist vantage point.

19. John Berger, *Ways of Seeing* (London: Penguin, 1972).

20. Robert J. Stoller, M.D., *Sex and Gender: On the Development of Masculinity and Femininity* (New York: Science House, 1968): 206–17.

21. Garber's *Vested Interests* provides a wealth of detail about cross-dressing practices—and our obsessed fascination with them.

Chapter Three

1. Irvin Yalom, M.D., *Love's Executioner* (New York: Basic Books, 1989): 88.

2. See *Shadow on a Tightrope: Writings by Women on Fat Oppression*, Lisa Schoenfielder and Barb Wieser, eds. (San Francisco: Spinster Press, 1983).

3. Gina Kolata, "Women Pay High Price for Being Overweight," *New York Times* (October 30, 1993).

4. Susan Bordo, *Unbearable Weight: feminism, Western culture, and the body* (Berkeley: University of California Press, 1993): 185–212.

5. Anne Hollander, "When Fat Was in Fashion," *New York Times Magazine* (October 23, 1977): 122. See also Anne Hollander, *Seeing Through Clothes* (New York: Viking, 1978).

6. Hollander, "When Fat Was in Fashion," 36.

7. Gina Kolata, "Burdens of Being Overweight," *New York Times* (November 22, 1992).

8. One study estimated that for every pound overweight businessmen too lose a thousand dollars a year in salary. Kolata, "Burdens of Being Overweight."

9. Robert Sherrill, "Phil Gramm's Trail of Sleaze," *The Nation* (March 6, 1995): 301.

10. Marcia Millman, *Such a Pretty Face: Being Fat in America* (New York: Berkley, 1980).

11. Kolata, "Burdens of Being Overweight."

12. Kolata, "Burdens of Being Overweight."

13. Lesbian historian Lillian Faderman, quoted in Natalie Angier, "Research on Sex Orientation Doesn't Neatly Fit the Mold," *New York Times* (July 18, 1993).

14. Robert Hughes, *Culture of Complaint: The Fraying of America* (New York: Warner, 1993).

15. See Lauren Berlant, "The Female Complaint," *Social Text* *19–20* (Fall 1988); also "America, 'Fat,' the Fetus," *boundary 2* (Fall 1994): 145–95.

16. "The Jerry Springer Show," "Fat Greeting Cards" (September 16, 1994). Transcription by Burrelle's Information Services.

17. Patrick Brantlinger, *Bread and Circuses: Theories of Mass Culture as Social Decay* (Ithaca: Cornell University Press, 1983); also see Andrew Ross, *No Respect: Intellectuals and Popular Culture* (New York: Routledge, 1989).

18. Ian Hacking discusses these debates in *Rewriting the Soul: Multiple Personalities and the Science of Memory* (Princeton, N.J.: Princeton University Press, 1995): 250–54.

19. Susan Stewart, *On Longing: Narratives of the Miniature, the Gigantic, the Souvenir, the Collection* (Durham, N.C.: Duke University Press, 1993).

Chapter Four

1. Officials said they were troubled by inconsistencies in the evidence and didn't take the case to trial. Franklin has been convicted of killing interracial couples in Utah and Wisconsin and linked to thirteen racially motivated killings across the country, including the shooting of civil rights leader Vernon Jordan.

2. Hunt, *The Invention of Pornography*, 10–30.

3. For biographical information on Flynt I've drawn on Robert Ward, "Grossing out with Publishing's Hottest Hustler," *New Times* (January 9, 1976); Rudy Maxa, "Behind the Steel Door," *California Magazine* (June 1983); Jeffrey Klein, "Born Again Porn," *Mother Jones* (February/March 1987); and Tom Johnson, "The Hustler," *Los Angeles* (April 1987). Flynt's life and his legal travails have also been widely covered in the national press.

4. The Supreme Court's 1973 ruling on obscenity allowing communities to set their own standards for offensiveness meant that separate suits could be brought against pornographers for obscenity by any locality around the country.

5. Interestingly, the FCC's decision in Flynt's case is now being deployed as a precedent by antiabortion candidates who want to run campaign ads featuring graphic footage of bloody, aborted fetuses.

6. Mikhail Bakhtin, *Rabelais and His World* (Bloomington: University of Indiana Press, 1984). My reading of *Hustler* owes much to Bakhtin's dazzling analysis of the politics of the grotesque.

7. *Newsweek* (February 16, 1976): 69.

8. Bakhtin, 376.

9. Mary Douglas, *Natural Symbols: Explorations in Cosmology* (London: Barrie & Rockliff, 1970): 70.

10. Peter Stallybrass and Allon White, *The Politics and Poetics of Transgression* (Ithaca: Cornell University Press, 1986). Stallybrass and White don't write on pornography specifically, but the influence of their work very much shapes this chapter, as it does my general understanding of pornography throughout the book.

11. Stallybrass and White, chapters 1 and 5.

12. See Norbert Elias, *History of Manners* (New York: Pantheon, 1978).

13. Several writers who have visited the *Hustler* offices testify that (to their surprise) these sorts of letters *are* sent by actual readers; at its peak circulation *Hustler* received well over a thousand letters a month. As to whether this particular letter was written by a reader or a staff writer, I have no way of knowing, but it's typical of the *Hustler* worldview.

14. Stallybrass and White, 191.

15. Elias, 120.

16. Andrea Dworkin, *Intercourse* (New York: Free Press, 1987): 187.

17. Dworkin, along with Catharine MacKinnon, is the author of antipornography legislation that a number of municipalities around the country have attempted to enact.

18. There are ongoing attempts to regulate this sort of imagery. During the controversies over National Endowment for the Arts funding for artists, a Republican representative attempted to introduce a bill in Congress that would prohibit public funding of art that depicts aborted fetuses. This was something of a shortsighted strategy, as the aborted fetus has been, of course, a favored incendiary image of antiabortion forces. *New York Times* (October 10, 1990): 6.

19. Mary Douglas, *Purity and Danger: An Analysis of the Concepts of Pollution and Taboo* (London: Routledge, 1966): 37.

20. Dworkin, 138.

21. Douglas, *Purity and Danger*, 3.

22. Dworkin, 187.

23. As for Catharine MacKinnon and Andrea Dworkin, even if they don't strictly reject social constructionism, their social descriptions, particularly of male sexuality, have a tendency to fall back on what sound like biologically based and essentialist notions of masculinity and femininity.

24. Laplanche and Pontalis, *The Language of Psychoanalysis*, 376–78.

25. *Hustler*'s advertising consists almost entirely of ads for sex toys, sex aids, porn movies, and phone sex services, as the automobile makers, liquor companies, and manufacturers of other upscale items that constitute the financial backbone of *Playboy* and *Penthouse* refuse to hawk their wares in the pages of *Hustler*. Flynt also early on rejected cigarette ads, both because he's adamantly antismoking and probably because numerous *Hustler* cartoons consist of grisly cancer jokes. In order to survive financially, *Hustler* began, among other enterprises, its now hugely successful magazine distribution company.

26. After yet another legal entanglement, *Hustler* began threatening in its model release form to prosecute anyone who sent in a photo without the model's consent. They now demand photocopies of two forms of ID for both age and identity purposes; they also stopped paying the photographer and began paying only the model.

27. Because *Hustler* doesn't subsist on advertising, its readership demographics aren't made public, making speculation about the actual class position of its readers unreliable at best. *Mother Jones* magazine did obtain and publish *Hustler*'s 1976 demographics, which were made available to them because Larry Flynt was courting *Mother Jones* for his distribution stable. Jeffrey Klein writes, "Originally it was thought that *Hustler* appealed to a blue-collar audience yet . . . demographics indicate that except for their gender (85 percent male), *Hustler* readers can't be so easily categorized. About 40 percent attended college; 23 percent are professionals; 59 percent have household incomes of $15,000 or more a year [about $38,000 in 1993 dollars], which is above the national mean, given the median reader age of 30." His analysis of these figures is, "Probably it's more accurate to say that *Hustler* appeals to what

people would like to label a blue-collar urge, an urge most American men seem to share." Klein, "Born Again Porn."

28. The story of the cover was related by Paul Krassner, who worked for *Hustler* in 1978, in "Is This the Real Message of Pornography?" *Harpers* (November 1984): 35. This cover was instrumental in the founding, the following year, of Women Against Pornography (WAP), the first feminist antipornography group. *Hustler*'s lack of joke sophistication seems to be its downfall, and if there's any truth to the cliché about feminists lacking a sense of humor, it may be that it's a class attribute as opposed to something inherent to feminism.

29. LFP Enterprises is a $100-million business, publishing about thirty different magazines and distributing over eighty more. Michael Kaplan, "The Resurrection of Larry Flynt; Owner of Larry Flynt Publications, Inc.," *Folio: The Magazine for Magazine Management* (June 15, 1993): 36.

Chapter Five

1. Hunt, *The Invention of Pornography*, 9–45.

2. On the relation of spanking to rhythm, specifically to poetry, see Eve Kosofsky Sedgwick, "A Poem Is Being Written," *Representations* (Winter 1987).

3. Adam Phillips, *On Kissing, Tickling and Being Bored* (Cambridge, Mass.: Harvard University Press, 1993): 9–11.

4. The first quote is in "The Dissolution of the Oedipus Complex" (1924), the second is in "On the Universal Tendency to Debasement in the Sphere of Love" (1912). Both essays can be

found in Sigmund Freud, *On Sexuality* (New York: Penguin, 1977): 259 and 320.

5. Elias, *The History of Manners,* 129–69.

6. See Raymond Williams, *Keywords: A Vocabulary of Culture and Society* (New York: Oxford University Press, 1976): 264–66; Elias also has much to say about taste throughout *The History of Manners*.

7. Gunshot wounds are the second leading cause of accidental death in the country after auto accidents, and these deaths have increased by 14 percent over the last ten years. There were 38,317 gunshot deaths in 1991. "Guns Gaining on Cars as Bigger Killer in U.S.," *New York Times* (January 28, 1995).

8. Edward Donnerstein and Daniel Linz, "Mass Media, Sexual Violence and Male Viewers: Current Theory and Research, *American Behavioral Scientist* 29 (May/June 1986): 601–18.

9. Carol Clover, *Men, Women and Chain Saws: Gender in the Modern Horror Film* (Princeton, N.J.: Princeton University Press, 1992): 139. Clover makes an extended analysis of *I Spit on Your Grave*; I borrow the term "rape-revenge film" from her.

10. The problem seems to be that men overreport and women underreport sexual activity. In the recent widely-publicized University of Chicago sex survey, 64 percent of male sexual contacts can't be accounted for—or rather, could be accounted for only if in this survey of 3,500 people, 10 different women each had 2,000 partners they didn't tell researchers about. To solve this problem, one statistician suggested eliminating from the data all respondents who reported having more than twenty sex

partners in their lifetime; she found if she eliminated all people who said they had more than five partners in the last year, the data made even more sense. David L. Wheeler, "Explaining the Discrepancies in Sex Surveys," *The Chronicle of Higher Education* (October 27, 1993): A9. This sounds less like crunching numbers than inventing them.

11. Keith Bradsher, "Gap in Wealth in U.S. Called Widest in West," *New York Times* (April 17, 1995), cites new studies reporting that the wealthiest 1 percent of Americans now own nearly 40 percent of the national wealth, that the gap between rich and middle class widened throughout the 1970s and 1980s, just as the new planned welfare cuts and tax breaks for the wealthy will further widen that gap and further impoverish the poor.

12. I've been much helped in thinking about the specifics of current economic shifts and their relation to cultural distinction-making by Roger Rouse's "Thinking Through Transnationalism: Notes on the Cultural Politics of Class Relations in the Contemporary United States," *Public Culture* (Winter, 1995): 353–402.

13. Roger Kimball, *Tenured Radicals: How Politics Has Corrupted Our Higher Education* (New York: Harper & Row, 1990): 145–46.

14. Allan Bloom, *The Closing of the American Mind: How Higher Education Has Failed Democracy and Impoverished the Souls of Today's Students* (New York: Simon & Schuster, 1987). For a scathing critique of Bloom's classical scholarship see Martha Nussbaum, "Undemocratic Vistas," *New York Review of Books* (November 5, 1987): 20–26.

15. Jonathan P. Hicks, "Giuliani Gets Accord on Sex-Shop Limits," *New York Times* (March 13, 1995).

16. Michel Foucault, *The History of Sexuality* (New York: Random House, 1978) is the source of this line of thinking.

17. James Kincaid, *Child-Loving: The Erotic Child and Victorian Culture* (New York: Routledge, 1992): 246–70.

18. *The Boston Globe*, January 28, 1992, reports Bloom's contributions to the *Harvard Peninsula*.

19. Eve Kosofsky Sedgwick, who was a student of Bloom's, reads him somewhat similarly in *Epistemology of the Closet* (Berkeley: University of California Press, 1990): 55–8.

   Although it was fairly common knowledge around the University of Chicago campus, where he taught, that Bloom was gay, he was closeted in his national career as best-selling conservative author (when he died in 1992, obituaries referred to him as a "lifelong bachelor"). Given that his public pronouncements and political affiliations seemed in conflict with his personal life, this was of some local interest. Thus inevitably, rumors swept the campus that he'd died of AIDS not, as the university announced, bleeding ulcers.

20. Dworkin, *Intercourse*, 138.

21. Strossen, *Defending Pornography*, 231–38.

22. These articles were later published as *In the Freud Archives* (New York: Knopf, 1984).

23. David Stout, in "A Child at Play and Malcolm's Missing Notes," *New York Times* (August 30, 1995), indicates that Masson plans yet another lawsuit.

24. These are recounted in *My Father's Guru* (Reading, Mass.: Addison-Wesley, 1993). The family took baths together, and under the sway of this guru, were devoted to hygiene practices like enemas.

25. My discussion of fantasy and psychical reality is drawn from Jean Laplanche and J.-B. Pontalis, "Fantasy and the Origins of Sexuality," *The International Journal of Psycho-Analysis* (Vol. 49, 1968): 1–18, in addition to Freud's own work.

26. Jeffrey Moussaieff Masson, *The Assault on Truth: Freud's Suppression of the Seduction Theory* (New York: Farrar, Straus and Giroux, 1984).

27. MacKinnon, *Only Words*: 9–41.

28. Jeffrey Masson, "Incest Pornography and the Problem of Fantasy," in *Men Confront Pornography*, Michael S. Kimmel, ed. (New York: Meridian, 1990): 142–52.

29. Clover, *Men, Women and Chain Saws*. See pages 21–64 on male identification with female characters.

30. Strossen, *Defending Pornography*.

31. There's been a lot of attention paid lately to the way pornography is transforming itself to appeal more to women viewers, and to the development of a new subgenre referred to as

"couples" porn, which focuses more on romance, foreplay, and mutuality. Just as the introduction of greater numbers of women into the work force has had a transforming effect on workplaces, the growing number of female pornography viewers has perhaps similarly "feminized" porn. As have growing numbers of women pornography makers, the most well known of whom is Candida Royalle, of Femme Productions. See Candida Royalle, "Porn in the USA," *Social Text* 37 (Winter 1993): 23–32.

32. I'm borrowing and revising the term from Thomas Laquer's use of the "one-sex" model to describe early theories of sexual difference. *Making Sex: Body and Gender from the Greeks to Freud* (Cambridge, Mass.: Harvard University Press, 1990).

33. Strossen points out that, in fact, most rape victims are actually men in prison: estimates are that more than twice as many men than women are raped per year. This suggests that anti-rape activists should focus on prison reform, not pornography, both to prevent rape behind bars and because it's likely that sexual assaults on men in prison translate into subsequent attacks on women outside prison. Strossen, 275.

Acknowledgments

I'm extraordinarily grateful for fellowships from the John Simon Guggenheim Foundation, and from the Rockefeller Foundation, which partly supported the writing of this book, and for a research grant from the Northwestern University Center for the Humanities, and for research support and leave from Northwestern's School of Speech. Thanks also to the Chicago Humanities Institute at the University of Chicago, where I was installed during the Rockefeller fellowship.

My biggest intellectual and personal debt is to Lauren Berlant: her own brilliant work on national culture and her laser-like, penetrating comments on the manuscript had enormous impact on my thinking, her friendship sustained me through various dark moments, her community standards are ones I aspire to emulate, and we've spent so many years discussing these things that I'm not sure where her ideas leave off and mine begin. Let me also thank people who kindly read and hashed over various parts of the book with me: Jonathan Black, Michelle Citron, Scott

Acknowledgments

Goodman, Barbara Fajardo, Nancy Fraser, Miriam Hanson, Phyllis Kaplan, Herb Kipnis, Chuck Kleinhans, Colin MacCabe, Jim Peterson, Roger Rouse, Candace Vogler, my mother, Myra Balesi, and especially, as always, Steve Rodby, for painstaking readings and many other forms of generosity and wonderfulness. Thanks to Tim Brennan, who overcame his Catholic upbringing and combed Times Square porn stores with me. My dad, Len Kipnis, read much of the manuscript and was a major support and enthusiast throughout the writing of it, and my sister, Nancy Goodman, was a rock in her own inimitable way. And thanks to both my parents for that fruitful combination of neurosis, ambition, and transitory optimism that impelled me to write this.

Audiences at the University of Michigan, State University of New York at Buffalo, University of Chicago, Northwestern, the 1994 Society for Cinema Studies Conference at Syracuse University, the School of the Art Institute of Chicago, the University of Florida in Gainesville, the Kulturhaus in Linz, Austria, the Chicago Film Seminar, and the University of Wisconsin-Madison television colloquium also offered helpful and interesting comments on drafts of various chapters.

For the writing of chapter 1, I'd like to thank Daniel DePew, who unconditionally subjected himself to my interrogatories, attorney James Lowe, who turned over his vast files on the case and was extremely generous with his time and assistance, and Mike Lamitie of Ray Brook Federal Correctional Institution for official courtesy and unexpected kindness.

And finally, grateful thanks to Diana Finch, my most wonderful agent, and to my very smart editor, Allison Draper, both of whom improved the book considerably and were very sweet along the way.

363.4 **Kipnis, Laura.**
Kip
            Bound and gagged.

DATE			